The Seven Gifts *of the* Holy Spirit

Other Liguori Titles
by Mitch Finley

The Catholic Virtues:
Seven Pillars of a Good Life

For Men Only:
Strategies for Living Catholic

The Ten Commandments:
Timeless Challenges for Today

Saint Anthony and Saint Jude:
True Stories of Heavenly Help

101 Ways to Happiness:
Nourishing Body, Mind, and Soul

The Heart and Soul of Imitating Christ:
A Fresh Look at the Thomas à Kempis Classic

The Corporal and Spiritual Works of Mercy:
Living Christian Love and Compassion

The Seven Gifts of the Holy Spirit

Mitch Finley

Liguori
LIGUORI, MISSOURI

Published by Liguori Publications
Liguori, Missouri
www.liguori.org

Library of Congress Cataloging-in-Publication Data
Finley, Mitch
    The seven gifts of the Holy Spirit / Mitch Finley. — 1st ed.
    p. cm.
    ISBN 978-0-7648-0719-0
    1. Holy Spirit. 2. Gifts, Spiritual. I. Title.
BT121.2 .F49 2001
234'.13—dc21   00-050649

Liguori Publications, a nonprofit corporation, is an apostolate of the Redemptorists. To learn more about the Redemptorists, visit *Redemptorists.com*.

Printed in the United States of America
17 16 15 14 13 / 11 10 9 8 7

Contents

Introduction

What or Who Is the Holy Spirit, and What Gifts Why?

We can't talk about God in a Christian context with-out talking about the one God as the Holy Trinity. To use the traditional metaphors: Father, Son, and Holy Spirit. This means that Christian talk about God must include the Holy Spirit, traditionally the third "Person" of the Trinity. In the words of theologian Barbara Finan, "Belief in the one God who is Father, Son, and Spirit is the central truth of all Christian theology and the core reality of Christian living."1

Thus, for discussion purposes, we can distinguish but not separate the Holy Spirit from God the Father and God the Son. Before we go any further, however, it is essential to remember that all religious language is metaphorical and analogical—that is, religious language is about realities that the human mind can never fully grasp, so we must rely on metaphors and analogies that we cannot take completely at face value. To quote the *Catechism of the Catholic Church*:

> Since our knowledge of God is limited, our language about him is equally so. We can name God only by taking creatures as our starting point, and in accordance with our limited human ways of knowing and thinking….
>
> Human words always fall short of the mystery of God.2

The one God is not literally "Father," "Son," and "Holy Spirit." These are simply traditional metaphors that, for some two thousand

years, have carried meaning about God believed by the Christian
churches to be most consistent with a Christian faith experience.3
These metaphors are inadequate, to be sure. Nevertheless, they
carry some truth about God and about the Christian experience of
God, so they are much better than no words at all. "Admittedly,"
the *Catechism* says, "in speaking about God like this, our language
is using human modes of expression; nevertheless it really does
attain to God himself, though unable to express him in his infinite
simplicity."4

This book is about the Holy Spirit, so for purposes of discussion I will distinguish the Holy Spirit from the other two Persons
in the Trinity. Who, or what, is this Holy Spirit, and why should we
care? What difference does the Holy Spirit make in our lives? To
put the question another way: So one Person in the Trinity is the
Holy Spirit. Time for that critical, frequently overlooked theological question: *So what?*

We have more than enough to be concerned about without caring one way or another about the Holy Spirit, right? Let theologians
and others inclined to get excited about theories and abstractions
care about the Holy Spirit. We have a living to make, work to do,
busy lives, bills to pay, family responsibilities. We can get along just
fine, thank you, without caring about the Holy Spirit. We'll wait
until the great by-and-by to find out about the Holy Spirit, no offense intended....

No offense taken, God surely responds. Can we imagine God
asking us, "Am I the Holy Trinity? Yes...and no. Is it true that one
of my 'Persons' is the 'Holy Spirit'? Yes...and no. Does it matter
whether you care about me, the Creator of the universe, as the
Holy Spirit? No...and yes."

It matters only if we care about love, peace, and joy. Only if,
sometimes in quiet moments, we wonder about the mystery of everything from our own existence to the existence of those we love
most. Only if we sometimes wonder why there is anything at all.
Only if we wonder where we and those we love came from. Only

if we wonder why we and those we love must die. Then, God says, we might want to give some thought to this "Holy Spirit" business.

If you have ever witnessed the birth of a child or the death of someone you love—if you have ever known the deep goodness of shared physical pleasure in a loving, lasting marriage—if you have ever been touched by the words of Scripture—or if a liturgy ever nourished you in places you had forgotten you had—if the words of a friend were ever just the words you needed most to hear—if you have ever felt deeply at peace for no apparent reason—if you have ever vented your anger directly to God and been relieved and a little surprised at how right it felt—if you have ever been able to pray when prayer seemed impossible—then you might want to learn more about the Holy Spirit.

At celebrations of the Eucharist on Sundays and holy days, Catholics pray the Nicene Creed, which includes the most explicit statement of Christian belief in the Holy Spirit:

> I believe in the Holy Spirit, the Lord, the giver of life,
> who proceeds from the Father and the Son,
> who with the Father and the Son is adored and glorified,
> who has spoken through the prophets.
> I believe in one, holy, catholic and apostolic Church.
> I confess one Baptism for the forgiveness of sins
> and I look forward to the resurrection of the dead
> and the life of the world to come.

Notice that it is belief in the Holy Spirit that gives rise to belief in the Church. Notice, too, that there are two ways to understand the phrase "believe in." First, it can mean that we accept and acknowledge the reality of the Holy Spirit and the reality of the Church. Second, "believe in" can mean that it is *in* the Holy Spirit that we find it possible to believe or have faith. It is *in* the Church that we find ourselves able to believe or have faith. It is *in* the Holy Spirit and *in* the Church that we find it possible to "acknowledge one baptism for the forgiveness of sins" and "look for the resurrection of the dead, and the life of the world to come."

It is the Holy Spirit who actually creates the Church, bringing us together as a community of believers, a people of God, the Body of Christ. It is the Holy Spirit who "facilitates" the ongoing process of salvation, the spiritual healing and liberation beginning in this world through baptism. The Holy Spirit is active in we who are the Church as the source of our union with one another. The Holy Spirit gives us, even now, the beginnings of the eternal life we have through our mystical and real intimacy with the risen Christ.

All forms of human intimacy and human unity come from the Holy Spirit present in us, healing and liberating us. We might say that the Holy Spirit is the Master of Surprises and the Cup of Overflowing. When we least expect salvation (spiritual healing and liberation), the Holy Spirit brings it to us in the most unexpected times and places. When we are most empty, the Holy Spirit fills us to capacity and beyond—although, paradoxically, sometimes "full" feels much like "empty."

According to Saint Paul, the Holy Spirit is the source of the greatest gifts and ministries:

> Now there are varieties of gifts, but the same Spirit; and there are varieties of services, but the same Lord; and there are varieties of activities, but it is the same God who activates all of them in everyone. To each is given the manifestation of the Spirit for the common good. To one is given through the Spirit the utterance of wisdom, and to another the utterance of knowledge according to the same Spirit, to another faith by the same Spirit, to another gifts of healing by the one Spirit, to another the working of miracles, to another prophecy, to another the discernment of spirits, to another various kinds of tongues, to another the interpretation of tongues. All these are activated by one and the same Spirit, who allots to each one individually just as the Spirit chooses (1 Corinthians 12:4–11).

The crucial sentence here is "To each is given the manifestation of the Spirit for the common good." The gifts we receive from the Holy Spirit are not for private purposes; rather, they are for the good of the entire community of faith and of the world at large. Indeed, the test of whether a gift is from God is whether it contributes to "the common good" and edifies the community. (Notice, by the way, the clear suggestion of the Trinity in this passage: "Spirit"… "Lord"…"God" in verses 4–6.)

The list of gifts Saint Paul gives us—wisdom, knowledge, faith, healing, miracles, prophecy, discernment of spirits, "tongues" (in Greek, *glossolalia*), and interpretation of tongues includes only two of the seven on the traditional list that this book is about, namely, *wisdom* and *knowledge*.

The book of the prophet Isaiah, in the Hebrew Scriptures or Old Testament, contributes five gifts to the list and repeats two of them: "The spirit of the LORD shall rest on him [for Christians, a reference to Jesus], the spirit of *wisdom* and *understanding*, the spirit of *counsel* and might, the spirit of *knowledge* and the *fear of the* LORD. His delight shall be in the *fear of the* LORD" (11:2–3a; emphasis added).

This leaves two gifts on the traditional list not accounted for: *fortitude* and *piety*. *Piety* is actually a particular translation of the first mention of "fear of the lord" in the passage from Isaiah. In the Septuagint, the second-century B.C. Greek translation of the Old Testament, "piety" was added to the list in Isaiah as a seventh gift, the biblical number "seven" being symbolic of plenitude, or fullness.

For the origins of *fortitude*, we must turn to the much later writings of theologians. Saint Thomas Aquinas, in particular, made important contributions to the development of the seven gifts as a theme in medieval theological reflections on the Holy Spirit.[5]

It is important, at this point, to realize that the Holy Spirit is not simply a name for a way in which God acts. When we talk about the Holy Spirit, we refer to a distinct "Person"—not merely a certain *mode* of God's action but a distinct *personal presence*.[6] This is a mystery within a mystery—meaning not a tough nut to be cracked, but a real experience we can never fully understand.

Rather than plodding further into an historical investigation, let's briefly consider some contemporary reflections on the meaning of the seven gifts of the Holy Spirit.

Especially since the Second Vatican Council, in the mid-1960s, Roman Catholic theology has emphasized the unity of the human person, holding that the whole person is touched and transformed by the Holy Spirit, especially through the sacraments of initiation: baptism, Eucharist, and confirmation. At the same time, there has been a shift away from viewing the person as an isolated individual, with a greater focus on the faith community.

Contemporary Roman Catholic theology tends to understand the gifts of the Holy Spirit in the context of grace—God's self-gift understood as a personal love relationship with God, a relationship that is deeper than the human intellect can ever grasp. The gifts of the Holy Spirit come to us, also, in the context of ongoing conversion, an "in proc- ess" reorientation of one's life away from self-centered concerns and toward the love of God and neighbor. This ongoing conversion is personal, to be sure, but it also extends to the transformation of this world's social values, institutions, and systems, including economic systems.

Finally, the Holy Spirit is the source of the Church's unity, that is, the unity of all who make up the Church. Yet as Saint Paul clearly suggests in the words from 1 Corinthians quoted on pages x–xi, this unity includes distinct roles within the community. It is also true that the Holy Spirit brings about diversity in unity. Unity does not necessarily mean uniformity in all things.

Legitimate diversity is not the same as divisiveness. Where does a diversity that is from the Holy Spirit end and divisiveness begin? Divisiveness, within the Roman Catholic Church and among Christian denominations, is a sign that we lack the fullness of the Holy Spirit.

The fullness of the gifts of the Holy Spirit resides only in the risen Christ, of course. It is through our real and mystical union with Christ that we ourselves receive and experience these seven gifts. Thus, the heart of this book's message will be a reaffirmation of the ongoing need to nourish our relationship with Christ through the Church. In particular, we need to remind ourselves regularly of the importance of the sacraments as basic to the living of a Catholic spirituality and a Christian life in the world. Through frequent celebration of the Eucharist and reception of holy Communion, and by the daily practice of prayer and intimacy with the word of God in the Scriptures, we nourish intimacy with the Holy Spirit and the Spirit's seven gifts in us.

The seven gifts of the Holy Spirit are ways to understand the effects of the Holy Spirit's presence in the Church, in the persons who make up that community, and in the world at large. Keeping all this in mind, then, we move along to the main purpose of this book: reflections on the meaning and purpose of the seven gifts of the Holy Spirit, and some practical ways we can cultivate those gifts.

CHAPTER ONE

The Gift of Wisdom

We hear the word *wisdom,* and our inclination is to think of a form of knowledge that gives us all the information we need to make smart or clever choices. Wisdom comes with much life experience, we think. Wisdom is an old man or woman with nodding head and placid demeanor, unruffled by the world but sharp as a tack, ready with the perfect aphorism for any occasion.

Wisdom makes it possible for us to see all sides of an issue and make the correct choice—or so we think. If we are wise, we can stand apart from any situation or issue, ponder for a while, and then speak words that blow everyone right out of the water with their simplicity and depth of insight. If we are "wise," we can see below the surface to the heart of the matter, no matter what the matter is.

Old Testament Understanding of Wisdom

This understanding of *wisdom* is correct, as far as it goes. But there is far more to wisdom than being savvy, shrewd, or sharp. The Hebrew Scriptures emphasize that wisdom is highly desirable, but Old Testament documents also make it clear that true wisdom is not easy to obtain. In the Old Testament, *wisdom* is a translation of the Hebrew *hokmâ,* a feminine noun. Indeed, the Book of Proverbs metaphorically personifies wisdom in various positive female roles:

> Get wisdom; get insight: do not forget, nor turn away from the words of my mouth. Do not forsake her, and she will keep you; love her, and she will guard you (Proverbs 4:5–6).

It is Wisdom herself who speaks in Proverbs—and speaks as a prophet, one who brings the word of God—which, ultimately, is what wisdom is. In Proverbs 1–6, Wisdom is a woman of high social status who commands a messenger at will. Wisdom also appears as a "sister"—which has two meanings. Wisdom is a "sister" in the literal sense, meaning an immediate blood relative. But Wisdom is also a "sister" in the sense that she may be a woman with whom a man may relate as a wife or lover. In Proverbs, both the ideal wife (31:10) and the woman Wisdom (3:15, 8:11) are "more precious than jewels."

Proverbs 4:6 admonishes the listener not to forsake Wisdom, just as Proverbs 5:15–17 demands fidelity in marriage. Like women in ancient Israel who were wives and mothers, Wisdom is a counselor and teacher:

> Take my instruction instead of silver, and knowledge rather than choice gold; for wisdom is better than jewels, and all that you may desire cannot compare with her. I, wisdom, live with prudence, and I attain knowledge and discretion" (Proverbs 8:10–12).

Wisdom is regularly described as a life-giver or life-preserver. "Long life is in her right hand…" (Proverbs 3:16a). But remarkably, she is never portrayed as a child-bearer. Wisdom gives birth to no children.

Sometimes, it is difficult to distinguish clearly between Wisdom and God. For example, without the introductory verses to Proverbs 1:20–33, one might assume that the speaker is God rather than Wisdom:

> Wisdom cries out in the street; in the squares she raises her voice. At the busiest corner she cries out; at the entrance of the city gates she speaks:
>
> "How long, O simple ones, will you love being simple? How long will scoffers delight in their scoffing and fools hate knowledge? Give heed to my reproof; I will pour out my thoughts to you; I will make my words known to you. Because I have called and you refused, have stretched out my hand and no one heeded, and because you have ignored all my counsel and would have none of my reproof, I also will laugh at your calamity; I will mock when panic strikes you, when panic strikes you like a storm, and your calamity comes like a whirlwind, when distress and anguish come upon you. Then they will call upon me, but I will not answer; they will seek me diligently, but will not find me. Because they hated knowledge and did not choose the fear of the LORD, would have none of my counsel, and despised all my reproof, therefore they shall eat the fruit of their way and be sated with their own devices. For waywardness kills the simple, and the complacency of fools destroys them; but those who listen to me will be secure and will live at ease, without dread of disaster."

In fact, Wisdom is not God. For one thing, the Hebrew Scriptures never refer directly to God as feminine, either as "God" or under any other name.[1] Rather, Wisdom is God's created, feminine companion before creation:

The LORD created me at the beginning of his work, the first of his acts of long ago. Ages ago I was set up, at the first, before the beginning of the earth. When there were no depths I was brought forth, when there were no springs abounding with water. Before the mountains had been shaped, before the hills, I was brought forth—when he had not yet made earth and fields, or the world's first bits of soil. When he established the heavens, I was there, when he drew a circle on the face of the deep, when he made firm the skies above, when he established the fountains of the deep, when he assigned to the sea its limit, so that the waters might not transgress his command, when he marked out the foundations of the earth, then I was beside him, like a master worker; and I was daily his delight, rejoicing before him always, rejoicing in his inhabited world and delighting in the human race (Proverbs 8:22–31).

If we are alert to the nuances of this passage, we may notice that there are some interesting similarities to this portrayal of Wisdom and later New Testament ways of talking about Jesus as the Word (in Greek, *logos*), particularly in the Jo- han- nine and Pauline writings.

The theme of Wisdom the woman also appears in later Old Testament works such as the Wisdom of Solomon:

Wisdom is radiant and unfading, and she is easily discerned by those who love her, and is found by those who seek her. She hastens to make herself known to those who desire her. One who rises early to seek her will have no difficulty, for she will be found sitting at the gate. To fix one's thought on her is perfect understanding, and one who is vigilant

on her account will soon be free from care, because
she goes about seeking those worthy of her, and she
graciously appears to them in their paths, and meets
them in every thought (6:12–16).

The Book of Sirach:

> To fear the Lord is the beginning of wisdom; she is
> created with the faithful in the womb (1:14).

Sirach also equates Wisdom with the creative word of God
(24:3)—yet another anticipation of the fourth gospel—and
with the Torah (24:23), the entire body of Jewish religious
law and learning, including both sacred literature and oral
tradition.

Finally, the Book of the prophet Baruch equates the
woman, Wisdom, with the authentic knowledge necessary
for life:

> You have forsaken the fountain of wisdom.
> If you had walked in the way of God, you would
> be living in peace forever. Learn where there is wis-
> dom, where there is strength, where there is under-
> standing, so that you may at the same time discern
> where there is length of days, and life, where there
> is light for the eyes, and peace.
> Who has found her place? And who has entered
> her storehouses?...Later generations have seen the
> light of day, and have lived upon the earth; but
> they have not learned the way to knowledge, nor
> understood her paths, nor laid hold of her. Their
> descendants have strayed far from her way. She has
> not been heard of in Canaan, or seen in Teman; the
> descendants of Hagar, who seek for understanding on

the earth, the merchants of Merran and Teman, the story-tellers and the seekers for understanding, have not learned the way to wisdom, or given thought to her paths (3:12–23).

New Testament Understanding of Wisdom

Moving into the New Testament, we see that Saint Paul calls Christ "the wisdom (in Greek, *sophia*) of God" (1 Corinthians 1:24), and he makes it clear for the first time that true wisdom comes only from the Spirit:

> But we speak God's wisdom, secret and hidden, which God decreed before the ages for our glory. None of the rulers of this age understood this; for if they had, they would not have crucified the Lord of glory. But, as it is written, "What no eye has seen, nor ear heard, nor the human heart conceived, what God has prepared for those who love him" [see Isaiah 64:4]—these things God has revealed to us through the Spirit; for the Spirit searches everything, even the depths of God (1 Corinthians 2:7–10).

The prologue to the Gospel of John evokes Proverbs 8:22–28, quoted above, but it substitutes "Word" for "Wisdom," thus making the final identification between Christ as Wisdom and as God's Word:

> In the beginning was the Word, and the Word was with God, and the Word was God.
> He was in the beginning with God. All things came into being through him, and without him not one thing came into being. What has come into be-

ing in him was life, and the life was the light of all
people (1:1–4).

Together, then, Saint Paul and the redactor of the Gospel of
John establish the Christian notion that wisdom comes from
the Spirit and that wisdom is none other than God's own
Word who became incarnate in Christ. From now on, when
we speak of "wisdom," therefore, it must be as the gift of
the Spirit and not as an impersonal "force" or "influence,"
or even as a "virtue," but as Christ present and active in all
of us through the presence and power of the Holy Spirit.

How Does Wisdom Help Us Know God's Will?

Lest we fall into the pit of our own theoretical extrapola-
tions, however, we need to ask that important theological
question again: So what? So we receive the gift of wisdom,
which is the presence of Christ in us. So what?

The gift of wisdom is the gift of being able to think and
act in ways that will give us a life worth living. Wisdom is
knowledge, yes, but knowledge in the sense that it helps us
know what to do and say in order to act and speak in ways
consistent with God's will.

Right away, however, we need to sidestep a mistake
people often make when they think of "God's will." Sometimes we have an unrealistic understanding of the concept
of "the will of God." We have a general idea, for example,
that: it is God's will that we love our neighbor as we love
ourselves, and so forth. But we don't know what exactly
God wants us to do with this life, say. It's a real puzzler,
trying to figure out God's will.

But this is not how God's will works. Through the gift
of wisdom we come to know God's will not by hours, days,

or weeks of knocking on heaven's door until God finally gives in and reveals the answer. Rather, wisdom enables us to know God's will by opening us to our own talents and skills, to opportunities, and to prayer, during which we ask the Holy Spirit to guide and enlighten us, that we may know what to do.

Wisdom changes seeking God's will from a "gotta crack this nut" kind of process to a "gotta be faithful to the journey" kind of process. For there is no "God's will once and for all" that we discover, and that resolves all our life issues, and what a relief it is to have *that* over with. Rather, learning and following "God's will" is an ongoing pilgrimage that often begins only once we've decided that a certain choice is God's will.

For example, say you decide that it's God's will for you to marry a certain person, or enter a religious community, or become a priest, or remain single for life. In one sense that settles a big question. But every day still brings many questions about how to be faithful to that choice. Ultimately, we make the choices, not God.

Even making the choice for marriage leaves other issues unsettled. Indeed, every time you work out "God's will" about something, you find yourself faced with a whole new set of questions. What is God's will when it comes to everyday efforts to nourish your marriage when work or career makes excessive demands?

The gift of wisdom helps us work through the process of discovering who we are and what we should be about, not just from our perspective but from God's perspective, too. In giving us a broader, deeper point of view, wisdom also helps us make choices based not just on our needs and desires but on the needs of others. Wisdom helps us to make choices based more on love of God and neighbor than on the natural tendency to be self-centered and self-protective.

Wisdom helps us see that we are called to be for others, regardless of who we are or the choices we make. We are called to paradox, to "fulfill self" only by being for others.

As well, wisdom helps us see and accept that God's will also includes a call to embrace the cross of Christ in some form or other. As Jesus said in the Gospel of Mark,

> If any want to become my followers, let them deny themselves and take up their cross and follow me. For those who want to save their life will lose it, and those who lose their life for my sake, and for the sake of the gospel, will save it (8:34–35).

The gift of wisdom helps us see that though these words of Jesus are words of eternal life, they are words to be lived in this life. Wisdom helps us see that the only path to fullness of life, in this life and the next, is the path of the cross—that is, living with such integrity that we can accept with tranquillity the consequences of who we are. At the same time, wisdom helps us embrace the truth that God created us to be people who use our talents in service to God and neighbor.

Wisdom Helps Us See God Everywhere

The gift of wisdom is the gift of being able to see not just with the eyes of the body but with the heart, and to hear God speaking in the heart words that the world thinks of as complete nonsense. Wisdom makes it possible to see and hear a truth to which the world is often blind and deaf, the truth of the gospel. Wisdom helps us fashion a life not according to the superficial standards of a consumer society but according to the eternal standards set by Christ.

Not to cast the world in too negative a light, however. We need to remember that the Son of God came into the world, so "the world" is in the process of being saved, too. "The world" is a mix of darkness and light, and it's important for believers to cultivate the ability to distinguish between the two and celebrate the light wherever it may be found, whether in explicitly religious or ordinary situations. There are even "secular" times and places in which God may be found more readily than in explicitly religious ones. Wisdom helps us recognize the holy in the ordinary. In other words, wisdom helps us overcome the sacred/secular dichotomy our culture takes for granted. Wisdom can read holy messages in the daily newspaper as easily as she can find the word of God in Scripture. Wisdom can find God in the middle of a supermarket as easily as in a church. Wisdom can feel God's joy in learning to play the five-string banjo as easily as she can feel God's joy in Beethoven's *Ninth Symphony.* Wisdom gives us a vision of the everyday world that makes it possible to find divine truths in John Steinbeck's *The Grapes of Wrath* as readily as in a papal encyclical. The point is not that the two are identical but that wisdom enables us to recognize authentic truth or authentic falsehood wherever we find it, in a novel or in an official Church document. A papal encyclical on social justice, for example, can make even more sense if we read *The Grapes of Wrath,* too.

Commonly, the holy takes us by surprise in family relationships, both the pleasant and the unpleasant, the warm and the cold. Couples experience God's love in a healthy, loving marriage so frequently that it can come to seem almost ordinary.

Paradoxically, the gift of wisdom makes it possible to take such moments for granted. God brings healing and forgiveness, and a deeper capacity for genuine love, into a marriage, and the spouses may not even recognize God's presence as extraordinary at the time. That, after all, is where God is and what God does.

The natural events of marriage and family life are so "primed" for little explosions of divine love and holiness that they can become almost a part of the everyday landscape. Parent-child relationships are ripe for such experiences. From the countless times husband and wife make love and no child is conceived to that one special time that leads, in an instant known only to God, to conception, the air is thick with God in joyful, sad, and everyday, ordinary times. Most often in retrospect, perhaps, wisdom enables us to recognize this, and may even send us to our knees with our faces to the ground in gratitude to the One whose love makes it all happen.

In the big, wider world, too, wisdom shows us goodness, beauty, and truth, all signs and manifestations of God's presence. From a Roman Catholic perspective, indeed, there is no place where and no time when it is not possible for God to be present to us. For God, we believe and experience, is in all places and all times always. Wisdom tells us so.

Think of the most ordinary, mundane, boring, or terrible situation you can imagine. God is there. Back in the early 1990s, *Pulp Fiction*, a film by Quentin Tarantino, hit the theaters and caused quite a stir. A series of short, obliquely related stories, *Pulp Fiction* includes considerable graphic violence and portrayals of human cruelty. In a very real sense, however, *Pulp Fiction* is a lesson about or illustration of the Catholic conviction that even in the darkest night there is a shining star someplace, if you look for it; that even the meanest, most rotten character retains the potential to act in an unselfish, loving manner. In each of the stories in *Pulp Fiction* there is a glimmer of goodness and hint of hope. Wisdom reveals that hint of goodness in the midst of an evil situation, that glimmer of hope in the midst of the most overwhelming hopelessness.

Wisdom gives us the ability to see other people as God sees them, not as the world sees them. With wisdom, we can look at someone the world regards as having little or no worth and see that person's infinite value from God's perspective. With wisdom, we can see God in, for example, a person with the most profound disabilities, a prisoner on death row, or a person with Alzheimer's or AIDS. Wisdom opens the heart to even the most marginalized people, those society regards as "dead weight," and shows us that they, too, are children of our God, who is closer to us than we are to ourselves.

Wisdom Illuminates the Truths of the Scriptures

One of Wisdom's most helpful benefits is the way she helps faith to sidestep simplemindedness in various forms. The Holy Spirit's gift of wisdom helps us use the brains God gave us when it comes to reading the Scriptures, for example, and shows how fundamentalist readings fail to do both God and God's word the justice they are due.

This is where it becomes clear that wisdom is similar to a natural talent. It doesn't develop automatically. If one has musical talent, for example, one needs to develop that talent through education and practice. In a similar fashion, the gift of wisdom requires that we gather the practical information we need to apply the gift. With regard to reading and interpreting the Scriptures, for example, we need to gain some basic information first—what the Scriptures are, where they came from, and so forth—before wisdom can guide us in reading and praying with them. If we choose to skip this step, wisdom won't save us from the pitfalls of scriptural misinterpretation. Wisdom isn't magic; it's a gift that needs to be developed and exercised.

Saint Thomas Aquinas called wisdom "a sort of judgment by sympathy in divine matters."[2] He also described wisdom as a "disposition of mind."[3] In other words, wisdom inclines us to use the old noggin in ways compatible with authentic faith, but we need to accumulate the material for the intellect to use when it comes to reading the Scriptures, for example. Wisdom says, "Read a couple of good books *about* the Bible, *then* read the Bible, and apply what you learned."

The same is true of any aspect of the Christian life. Wisdom inclines us to use common sense at all times. Say someone claims to be a spiritual guide or teacher, and then he or she advises us to sell all that we have, give away all of our money, and move to the Outer Maldives to await the Second Coming, which will be in a couple of months or so. The gift of wisdom rings a bell and says, "Now, wait just a darn minute, here. This teacher is a couple of fries short of a Happy Meal. I don't think we will do any such thing."

If a book suggests that the members of certain races or ethnic groups are not quite as good as the race or ethnic group we belong to, wisdom flashes a red light to warn us away. Wisdom is like a light in the darkness that prevents us from traveling blind in a world that has more than enough nonsense and foolish ideas to go around.

Wisdom Provides a Gospel Outlook on Living

Perhaps ultimately, the gift of wisdom enables us to maintain a gospel outlook on life and the world. In the Gospel of John, Jesus prays to his Father:

> I have given them your word, and the world has hated them because they do not belong to the world, just as

I do not belong to the world. I am not asking you to
take them out of the world, but I ask you to protect
them from the evil one. They do not belong to the
world, just as I do not belong to the world. Sanctify
them in the truth; your word is truth. As you have
sent me into the world, so I have sent them into the
world (17:14–18).

The traditional Roman Catholic way of summarizing the
way of "being in the world" that Jesus presents here is to
say that we are called to be "in but not of the world." In
other words, as disciples of Christ, we do not "belong to the
world," but we are "sent into the world" to live according to
God's word and to be a witness to the truth. Wisdom helps
us do this, to be fully "in the world" but not to "belong to
the world." We are called to be in and for the world, just as
Jesus was in and for the world, but according to the standards of the gospel. The gift of wisdom helps us to maintain
a balance between being "in" but "not of" the world. It
helps us to live "in-between" with the tension between the
two, without allowing us to go to either extreme.

The difficulty of living with this tension should not
be underestimated. Indeed, there are many examples of
Christians who flounder under the tension, giving in to the
attraction to be "in the world," as if there were no transcendent dimension to the gospel and to a Christian life in the
world. Christians heavily committed to social justice causes
sometimes adopt this position, overlooking in their outward
commitments the need for the sacraments and for prayer,
and acting as if everything depends on their own efforts.

Others go to the opposite extreme. They adopt a "fly
from the world and the things of the world" lifestyle. Prayer
and devotional practices become all-important, to the exclu-
sion of social concerns. Some tend to act as if everything
depends on prayer, and social and political activities are futile.

The truly Christian position is in the center, in that place of tension, maintaining a balance, "in and for, but not of, the world." Wisdom helps us live with that tension in creative ways, being both people of prayer and devotion and people of social justice. This is an example of one of the several ways in which Roman Catholicism is a "both/and" religion, not an "either/or" religion, and wisdom helps us hold it all together over the long haul.

Wisdom Is Mystery

For all that we can say about the gift of wisdom, however, there is no overcoming the fact that wisdom is the result of intimacy between infinite and finite, between God and us. We can experience wisdom in the heart, but it remains a mystery as far as the puny human intellect is concerned. Perhaps "Wisdom," a poem by Thomas Merton, says it best:

> *I studied it and it taught me nothing.*
> *I learned it and soon forgot everything else:*
> *Having forgotten, I was burdened with knowledge*
> *The insupportable knowledge of nothing.*
>
> *How sweet my life would be, if I were wise!*
> *Wisdom is well known*
> *When it is no longer seen or thought of.*
> *Only then is understanding bearable.*[4]

CHAPTER TWO

The Gift of Understanding

If we consult a dictionary about the definition of the word *understanding*, we will find something like this:

n. 1. The quality or condition of one who undestands; comprehension.

2. The faculty by which one understands; intelligence.

3. Individual or specified judgment or outlook; opinion.

4. A compact implicit between two or more people or groups. The matter implicit in such a compact.

5. A reconciliation of differences; a state of agreement: *They finally reached an understanding.*

6. A disposition to appreciate or share the feelings and thoughts of others; sympathy.

adj.1. Characterized by or having comprehension, good sense, or discernment.

2. Compassionate; sympathetic.[1]

This is a good example of a case in which the ordinary meaning of a word does not "rock 'n' roll" compared with the theological meaning of the same word. Here is one theo- logian's definition: "Understanding...is a gift for comprehending the things of life in relation to God and for achieving deeper insight into the truths held by faith. Self and others are seen as made in the image of God; in creation are discovered vestiges of God, which point to God the Creator."[2]

Understanding Makes a Difference in Our Everyday Lives

The theological definition of *understanding* is more precise and, at the same time, more limited than the ordinary definition. This is so because the theological definition confines itself to talking about *understanding* as a gift of the Holy Spirit, instead of including a mental or cognitive capacity, or an interpersonal situation or condition. The gift of the Holy Spirit that we call "understanding" is a way of seeing and thinking that results from faith, that is, from loving intimacy with the personal divine mystery we call "God." The gift of understanding, like the gift of wisdom, is a way of seeing with the heart, not just with our intellectual and rational parts.

Understanding helps us live from the heart while listening to the intellect, and vice versa: both ways of living are radically conditioned by faith. This is one way to summarize what the gift of understanding is about. As with most abstract theological statements, however, it takes more to truly understand this gift. We need to look to our own experiences before we begin to see how the gift of understanding makes a difference in our everyday lives and our everyday relationships with God and others.

Roman Catholicism, in particular, helps us do this because it is sacramental. As Catholics, we experience our faith not only on an intellectual level, not only on an emotional level, and certainly not as an abstraction. Rather, we experience and live our faith on every level of our existence. Our faith pays attention to the senses. Roman Catholicism is a "sensuous" religion. We like to touch, taste, and smell God—or, at least, we like to touch, taste, and smell God's presence.

We do this liturgically, of course, because the liturgy appeals to our senses. But we do it by being sensitive to God's presence in many other ways as well. We do it by being alert to God's presence in the natural world or in human relationships. We even see God moving in human activities, from politics to business, from technology to the arts. You name it, and Catholicism can find God there one way or another.

This sacramental way of being in the world makes it possible for Roman Catholics to "exercise" the gift of understanding in intellectual ways, sure. But it also makes it possible to apply understanding—seeing all things in the light of faith—on every level of existence. Thus, while Catholicism can sympathize with the simplicity of life embraced by Luddites, that is, those who oppose technological innovation, it can also find God in technological gadgets properly applied to human life. Catholics get as big a bang out of microchip technology as anyone because we see the Divine at work in microchips, too. The gift of understanding helps us see the hand of God at work everywhere, in human innovations as well as in the wonders of nature.

Does this mean that we accept, uncritically, every technological development that comes along? Does it mean that we celebrate every way in which technology is applied? In both cases, the answer is no. Catholicism has some serious problems with any form of technology that, by its very nature, destroys the fabric of human life or human communities. Take nuclear weapons, for example. Some argue that the simple existence of such weapons preserves peace; others, that it would always be immoral to use such weapons; still others, that it is immoral simply to possess or manufacture nuclear weapons, even if we never use them.

Take a much lower form of technical expertise, the manufacture and sale of tobacco products. There is virtually no sup- portable justification for making and selling a highly addictive product that, when used as it is designed to be used, is guaranteed to result in the early, lengthy, painful deaths of thousands of people every month. Sure, it takes years of nicotine addiction for cancer or emphysema to develop, but as the night follows the day, these early deaths do happen, so who can deny that the entire process is grossly immoral?

The *Catechism of the Catholic Church* includes tobacco among the things we should never "abuse."[3] A moment's reflection can lead to only one conclusion, however: that there is no common use of tobacco that is not an "abuse" because any of the common uses of tobacco are abuses of the human body and deleterious to human health. Sometimes smokers argue that they "enjoy" smoking or that smoking gives them pleasure or a sense of comfort. But the only "plea-sure" or "comfort" smokers get from smoking is the relief from painful addiction-withdrawal symptoms that results from giving the body more of the drug nicotine by smoking another cigarette. That's how an addiction works.

Roman Catholicism also opposes the *misuse* of technol-ogy. Television can be used in many good ways, but when it begins to erode the quality of family life, Catholicism says, "Whoa!" Computers have many beneficial applications, but when they are used to send pornography into our homes, Catholicism objects strenuously. Medical technology brings about many positive wonders, but when that same technol-ogy is used to directly end human life in the womb, or to carry out euthanasia, Catholicism says, "No way."

It is the gift of understanding that helps us see the difference between a good use of something dreamed up by the human mind and fashioned by human hands, and a misuse of the same thing. The Holy Spirit's gift of understanding gives the heart the capacity to "feel" its way through the forest of modern life, as it were. We live in a world filled with astonishments of many kinds, and understanding helps us view all things according to the standards of the gospel. Does this particular technology, for example, help people genuinely to love God and neighbor, or does it get in the way? Does this way to use this particular electronic or mechanical gadget serve real human needs, or does it take advantage of people and turn them into mere "consumers"?

Understanding Helps Us See God Everywhere

One of the greatest benefits of the gift of understanding is to fathom the presence of God in the most unlikely people and places. Just about anyone can see God in the face of a baby or a little child. But understanding helps us see God in the face of someone who is sick and dying, in the figure huddled in a doorway, in the person ravaged by cancer, in the angry, rebellious teenager…in the man dying a terrible death on a cross.

It's easy to see God in a beautiful sunset, but understanding helps us see God in an earthquake that wreaks destruction far and wide. It helps us understand the divine mystery of God's complete transcendence. Instead of using God as an easy explanation for just about anything, understanding helps us take seriously the dictum of Saint Thomas Aquinas to the effect that the first thing we need to say about God is that we can't say anything about God.

At the same time, understanding helps us register God's immanence, the radical extent to which God is *present*, as

Saint Augustine said, closer to us than we are to ourselves. In addition, understanding insists that we not limit God to either complete transcendence or complete immanence; rather, *both* remain completely true of God at all times. Understanding helps us live creatively in the tension of knowing God is both present and absent, near and far.

This benefit is no small thing. Countless people find it practically impossible to live with this tension, so they insist on thinking of God as *either* "way out there" or "closer than close." A God who is distant is much easier to ignore. A God who is close to the point of being snuggly can be turned into a kind of "lap dog" God, easy to take for granted. The trouble with both the distant God and the snuggly God is that sooner or later—usually sooner—they do not fit with our actual human experience of the real God.

A distant God can explain an earthquake: it means that God is uninvolved and couldn't care less. But a distant God makes no sense when it comes to the human experience of being loved unconditionally. A snuggly God can explain human love, but such a God no longer makes any sense when the one I love dies and, apparently, vanishes forever. Understanding helps keep us in touch with the real God who is simultaneously both absolute mystery and absolute love.

Understanding Helps Us Know Jesus As Human and Divine

Understanding has another explicitly Christian dimension, too. It stands us up, face to face, with Jesus the Christ who is both fully divine and fully human. In other words, this gift helps us take seriously the mystery of the Incarnation with all that it implies. Again, this is no small thing, nothing to take for granted. It can be difficult to tolerate living with such a mystery. It is much easier to believe that Jesus was simply God disguised as a man. Or that Jesus was a man who was so holy that he seemed to be divine. Only with the gift of understanding can we truly accept, with all its implications, that Jesus was, and is, "one divine person... possessing both a divine nature and a human nature."[4]

With the Holy Spirit's gift of understanding, we have no difficulty accepting the human nature of Jesus. We can believe, without batting an eyelash, that the Son of God came into the world as a helpless infant who brought delight to his mother, Mary, and his earthly father, Joseph. We can believe that Jesus had to grow "in wisdom and in years" (Luke 2:52) just as all humans do. With understanding, we have no problem accepting that Jesus experienced bodily existence as we do. He enjoyed a good meal, grew thirsty and tired, and exclaimed the first-century Palestinian equivalent of "ouch" when he stubbed his toe. Jesus was also a male human being, so he was psychologically male, he experienced a male body, and he experienced male feelings and emotions.

In fact, it is much easier to understand the humanity of Jesus than to understand his divinity and say what it meant during his earthly existence. Understanding helps us accept fully both Jesus' humanity and his divinity, but it does not mean that there is no more mystery. Rather, it means that the mystery becomes an affair of the heart more than of the intellect. We can connect with the simultaneity of Jesus' humanity and divinity in our deepest center because we do not need to understand into order to believe. Rather, because we believe, we can understand. Understanding is a result of our faith; it does not insist on preceding it.

In times past, the Roman Catholic emphasis was more on the divinity of Jesus, almost to the point that his humanity was not taken seriously. Today, if anything, the emphasis has shifted so that we may wonder what it means to say that the historical Jesus was divine as well as human. Humanity we can figure out—mysterious though it often is—at least we experience it ourselves, so we have a general idea of what Jesus' experience of his humanity must have been like. But how did Jesus experience his divinity? That's another issue entirely!

Understanding helps us look for the divinity of Jesus *in his humanity*. This is one approach, at least, and with understanding we can explore this perspective to see what it may reveal. Indeed, understanding tells us that any other perspective is bound to be mere abstract speculation. For it is only in his humanity—by means of the gospels, the living Christian tradition, and our experience of the risen Christ today—that we can know the God-man Jesus, and, in the process, never separate the two. So with understanding as our guide, let's see where a look at Jesus' humanity will lead. This may give us not only a clearer perspective on the gift of understanding but also a clearer vision of how Jesus' two natures influence our Christian faith.

First, the human nature of Jesus reveals his divine nature. This must be true, otherwise the gospels would not place such emphasis on Jesus' human nature. Mark, the oldest of the four gospels, tells the story of Jesus' baptism in order to emphasize his humanity:

> In those days Jesus came from Nazareth of Galilee and was baptized by John in the Jordan. And just as he was coming up out of the water, he saw the heavens torn apart and the Spirit descending like a dove on him. And a voice came from heaven, "You are my Son, the Beloved; with you I am well pleased" (1:9–11).

If Jesus were not human, it would make no sense for John to baptize him.

But for Mark, the "voice from heaven" reveals Jesus' divinity. The gift of understanding enables the redactor(s) of this gospel to record these words—indeed, the entire gospel—and it is only by means of understanding that we can read these words and let them sink into our hearts and change our lives from the inside out.

Take two other examples. The gospels of Matthew and Luke, unlike that of Mark, both include Infancy Narratives, accounts of the conception and birth of Jesus. Both communicate similar truths, but each has a unique approach. In Matthew, for example, Joseph plays a much more active role than he does in Luke. All the same, both emphasize the humanity of Jesus as well as his divinity. Matthew does this from the beginning of his gospel, when he states clearly that Jesus was born of a human mother but without the involvement of a human father: "When Joseph awoke from sleep, he did as the angel of the Lord commanded him; he took her as his wife, but had no marital relations with her until she had borne a son; and he named him Jesus" (1:24–25).

Luke makes the same point in his own way. In Luke we find the familiar account of the encounter between Mary and the angel Gabriel:

In the sixth month the angel Gabriel was sent by God to a town in Galilee called Nazareth, to a virgin engaged to a man whose name was Joseph, of the house of David. The virgin's name was Mary. And he came to her and said, "Greetings, favored one! The Lord is with you." But she was much perplexed by his words and pondered what sort of greeting this might be. The angel said to her, "Do not be afraid, Mary, for you have found favor with God. And now, you will conceive in your womb and bear a son, and you will name him Jesus. He will be great, and will be called the Son of the Most High, and the Lord God will give to him the throne of his ancestor David. He will reign over the house of Jacob forever, and of his kingdom there will be no end." Mary said to the angel, "How can this be, since I am a virgin?" The angel said to her, "The Holy Spirit will come upon you, and the power of the Most High will overshadow you; therefore the child to be born will be holy; he will be called Son of God..." (1:26–35).

Luke's account highlights Jesus' humanity by making it clear that he has a human mother. At the same time, there is no doubt about Jesus' divinity since he is conceived by the Holy Spirit and is "Son of the Most High."

In the fourth gospel, too, we find a presentation of Jesus' humanity and divinity, one that, again, echoes the unique way in which the human redactor(s) of John's gospel applied the Holy Spirit's gift of understanding. The fourth gospel places greater emphasis on Jesus' divinity than do the other three gospels. For example, in John's recounting of the last earthly days of Jesus, he shows us a Jesus who, in a sense, is in control at all times. Events unfold as they do only because he allows them to. Even at the moment of death, Jesus is in control. "Then he bowed his head and gave up his spirit" (19:30b), we read—a line not to be found in the other gospels.

All the same, the Gospel of John leaves no doubt about the humanity of the Son of God. Among the first words of this gospel we read, "And the Word became flesh and lived among us..." (1:14). Exercising the gift of understanding, the human author of these words has declared that it is precisely "the Word," that is, the divine person known as

Jesus, who "became flesh and lived among us." These few words sum up the mystery of the Incarnation as no other gospel does, and we are left with a truth that only the gift of understanding can enable us to accept.

In each case, the human redactor(s) of a gospel exercised the gift of understanding, but each wrote a unique gospel. Understanding does not lead to identical theological perspectives. This remains true today. The gift of understanding relates to the truth, but there are various ways to express truth.

Understanding Helps Us Belong to the Church

Roman Catholicism maintains that faith in Christ includes belonging to the community of faith. For Catholicism, one can't merely "accept Jesus Christ as your personal savior" and simply have an ongoing "Jesus and me" kind of faith. Rather, Roman Catholic faith requires active membership in the Church: the people of God, the Body of Christ. Understanding makes it possible to see this vital connection between faith and the Church. Here is how the Letter to the Ephesians expresses this:

> And [God] has put all things under [Christ's] feet and has made him the head over all things for the church, which is his body, the fullness of him who fills all in all (1:22–23).

In other words, faith in Christ is one with membership in the Church because the Church, in its innermost reality, *is* the Body of Christ. The gift of understanding shows us that to belong to Christ is to belong to this Church. Though other

Christian churches can manifest the Spirit of Christ in the world, it makes sense to want to belong to the faith community that traces its existence most directly to Christ and to his apostles, and that means the Roman Catholic Church. For the Catholic Church is the "mother church" of all the Christian churches. The gift of understanding makes it possible to see this intimate connection between Christ and the "one, holy, catholic, and apostolic" Church.

In its essence, the Catholic Church is a divinely established community of faith. At the same time, one doesn't need to look too long or too closely to see that as a human institution the Roman Catholic Church is far from perfect. We may believe that the Roman Catholic Church has the greatest *potential* to manifest the fullest expression of the Body of Christ in the world. But history shows that many of the human beings who have made up the Church down through the centuries have been far from saintly. Even many priests, bishops, and popes have failed at living the true spirit of the gospel; and, in our own time, it is easy to find people who have "left the Church" because they were hurt in some way by a member of the clergy or representative of a religious order. Others have stopped practicing the faith because they cannot agree with some official Church position or teaching.

Such cases are unfortunate—because the Holy Spirit's gift of understanding makes it possible to recognize the Church's imperfections, and the sins and imperfections of the Church's official representatives and leaders, and then to *see beyond* this "dark side." Understanding makes it possible to acknowledge that Christians are anything but perfect. One can use the sins and stupidity of other Church members as reason to stomp away from the Church and have nothing more to do with it. But understanding makes it possible to see that the imperfections—historically, sometimes the evil—that one finds in the Church do not negate the essence of what the Church is all about.

Understanding helps us see that while the Church has sheltered many sinners down through the centuries, it has also given birth to countless saints, many of whom started out as anything but saints. At the very least, it comes down to which is most significant, the Church's record on tolerating sinners or on cultivating saints.

Understanding helps us to be reasonable and fair about "the institutional Church's" flaws and failures. It helps us see that the only fair way to evaluate *any* human group, institution, or organization—including the Church—is to look closely at the ideals and goals the particular organization holds as its own. If we can admire and claim these as our own, then we can belong to that group.

If I base my evaluation of the Church on how successfully it lives out its ideals and goals, and if I insist on perfection in this regard, then I will never be able to accept the Church. The Church—meaning all the imperfect people who make up the Church—always has and always will fall short of its ideals. To reject the Church because many of its people are "hypocrites" is to imply that I am perfect myself and refuse to tolerate imperfection in any organization to which I would belong. In which case, I'm going to live a pretty lonely existence.

Yes, often the Church is a church of hypocrites, people who claim to believe that love of God and neighbor is what life is all about but who daily live as if other things are what life is all about. But at the same time, the Church is often a church of saints, people who truly act out of love for God and neighbor. The Church is that old reality, "a mixed bag," and understanding helps us see that what matters most about the Church is not that it sometimes does it wrong, but that it so often does it right.

Understanding helps us grasp the idea that the Church, just as we do, gains a better vision of the gospel as time goes by. With God's grace, the Church has a better, more accurate notion of what the gospel is all about today than it did at, say, the end of the nineteenth century. Therefore, the Church needs our patience and tolerance just as much as we need the patience and tolerance of others.

For centuries, during the Good Friday liturgy, Roman Catholics intoned a prayer for the "perfidious Jews." In 1959 Pope John XXIII, filled with the gift of understanding, interrupted the Mass to demand that the prayer be repeated without the offensive reference. From that time on, the word "perfidious" was eliminated from the Good Friday liturgy forever.[5]

Understanding enables us to see that the Church can, and does, change for the better sometimes. All the same, understanding helps us see that change for its own sake is no high ideal: sometimes the old things and the old ways are best, and sometimes they are not. Understanding helps us recognize when change brings the Church closer to the ideals of the gospel, and when it does not; when change brings *us* closer to the ideals of the gospel, and when it does not.

Understanding Reveals the Paradox of the Gospel

Without understanding, it is impossible to accept and live the paradox of the gospel precisely as a *paradox*. Take some words of Saint Ambrose (340–97), the bishop who had such a profound impact on Saint Augustine of Hippo (354–430):

The rich man who gives to the poor does not bestow alms but pays a debt.

The rule of justice is plain, namely, that a good man ought not to swerve from the truth, not to inflict any unjust loss on anyone, not to act in any way deceitfully or fraudulently.

How far, O rich, do you extend your senseless avarice? Do you intend to be the sole inhabitants of the earth? Why do you drive out the fellow sharers of nature, and claim it as for yourselves? The earth was made for all, rich and poor, in common. Why do you rich claim it as your exclusive right?[6]

Essentially, Saint Ambrose said, those who are rich—and the majority of those people living in the affluent nations of the developed world must think of themselves as "rich" today—have no special rights and no special power compared with those who are poor. In fact, Ambrose insisted that rich people have special obligations with regard to poor people. Think about it for a minute. These are words that make no sense apart from the paradox of the gospel, which reveals the rich as poor and the poor as rich. These words certainly make no sense in the context of modern life, in which wealth entitles one to be "more equal" than others. Only the gift of understanding makes it possible to take the words of Saint Ambrose seriously, to see the truth in what he said.

The gift of understanding helps us come closer to living and breathing the risen Christ in our everyday lives and in the everyday life of the Church. Understanding helps us see that, appearances to the contrary, our everyday lives *are* the life of the Church, both the joy and the anguish of it. For where we are, are Christ and the Church.

CHAPTER THREE

The Gift of Counsel

In the entire New Testament the word *counsel* occurs but twice. Here are those occurrences, each in its context. In each case, for our purposes, the word *counsel* is italicized. Also, the second example is longer, for reasons that will become evident soon:

> In Christ we have also obtained an inheritance, having been destined according to the purpose of him who accomplishes all things according to his *counsel* and will, so that we, who were the first to set our hope on Christ, might live for the praise of his glory (Ephesians 1:11–12).

> Let anyone who has an ear listen to what the Spirit is saying to the churches....
> I know your works; you are neither cold nor hot. I wish that you were either cold or hot. So, because you are lukewarm, and neither cold nor hot, I am about to spit you out of my mouth. For you say, "I am rich, I have prospered, and I need nothing." You do not realize that you are wretched, pitiable, poor, blind, and naked. Therefore I *counsel* you to buy from me gold refined by fire so that you may be

rich; and white robes to clothe you and to keep the shame of your nakedness from being seen; and salve to anoint your eyes so that you may see. I reprove and discipline those whom I love. Be earnest, therefore, and repent. Listen! I am standing at the door, knocking; if you hear my voice and open the door, I will come in to you and eat with you, and you with me. To the one who conquers I will give a place with me on my throne, just as I myself conquered and sat down with my Father on his throne. Let anyone who has an ear listen to what the Spirit is saying to the churches (Revelation 3:13 and 15–22).

At first sight, the Holy Spirit's gift of counsel may seem to have something to do with the modern idea of *counseling,* as in, "I need to get some counseling." In fact, the gift of counsel has only the remotest connection to this modern idea. To receive the gift of counsel does not mean that we become qualified to set up a "counseling practice." It does not mean that we may now offer all kinds of good advice to other people right off the top of our heads. Rather, as the two New Testament passages above suggest, the gift of counsel helps us to be open to the inspiration and guidance of the Holy Spirit.

More specifically, counsel opens us to the Spirit as we reflect, discern, consult, and advise in situations that have to do with teaching or taking specific actions.[1] Saint Thomas Aquinas says that we receive the gift of counsel to help us respond to what we believe "in particular situations."[2] In other words, our Christian faith is, first of all, the reality of our personal and communal relationship with the risen Christ. But we need the gift of counsel to help us discern how to apply or live out this relationship in specific situations.

The Gift of Counsel at Work: An Example

In her book *Traveling Mercies*, Anne Lamott has told the story of her gradual conversion to a "churchy" kind of faith—in her case, to the faith of a little Presbyterian church in Marin City, California. Lamott's story ends—or begins, depending on your point of view—with her belonging, in other words, to that bugaboo of modern popular culture, "institutional religion." Ultimately, Lamott had to rely on the gift of counsel as she made the choice to belong to this particular Christian community.

But the gift of counsel comes into play even in more day-to-day situations. It's not as if counsel arrives—ta-dah!—only when a significant "life choice" comes along. Lamott tells of a time when she went to a doctor for a physical checkup. The doctor noticed a mole on her rib cage and said, "There's something a little...*off* about this one." The doctor advised her to have the mole cut out and a biopsy done.

Calling herself "someone who is perhaps *ever* so slightly more anxious than the average hypochondriac," Lamott immediately began to worry.

"That night at bedtime I looked down at my mole, and now instead of it looking like a small sow bug, it suddenly seemed to be alive and spreading, like a stain. I was too young to die—or at least, I was too upset to die. You don't want to die when you're this upset—you get a bad room in heaven with the other hysterics...."

Thinking about heaven, however, made her remember that she believed in God. "And," she commented, "I smote my own forehead."

At this point, she decided to do something specific about her faith and about her situation, her nearly frantic fear that the biopsy would reveal that she had some horrible, incurable form of cancer. In other words, counsel "kicked in," and she determined that she could do something specific about her fear. "So," she explained, "I wrote God a note on a scrap of paper. It said, 'I am a little anxious. Help me remember that you are with me even now. I am going to take my sticky fingers off the control panel until I hear from you.'"

She then folded her note and dropped it into the drawer of the table next to her bed "as if it were God's In Box."3 Which, of course, is exactly what it was. Lamott's fear of cancer, and ultimately of death, made her think she was helpless, adrift on a shifting, uncontrollable sea of impending disaster. But counsel helped her see that no such thing was true. Counsel reminded her that she believed in God, which means that she believed in God's love. Then it helped her *do something in particular*: send a note to God.

That's how the gift of counsel works: it reminds us of things we already know. That we believe in God, that we are not without resources much greater than our fears, much greater than cancer, much greater, even, than death. Counsel reminds us that God's "in box" is right at hand, and all we need do is send God a note and the Creator of the universe, no less, will be at our service.

It's not as if counsel rids us of all anxiety, or gives us all the answers, or magically whisks us away to a place of no danger, above the mass of ordinary humanity. Lamott explained the difference that writing a note to God made for her:

A grown-up sort of peace came over me. I could feel it in the ensuing days, existing side by side with a heightened sense of symptoms. I developed pain in my upper jaw, which made me wonder what I would look like with most of my jaw removed...and then a burning spot in my stomach, which filled my head with scenes in which I was heroically full of good humor after the colostomy. But in between symptoms I felt pockets of trust and surrender, as if I had gone into total free fall and then landed gently after a drop of just a foot and a half.[4]

Counsel leads to "pockets of trust and surrender." Its purpose is not to work miracles but to remind us that God is right at our elbows, so to speak, and no matter what else happens we are not without resources and not without the ability to take action. We can write a note and put it in God's in box. We can turn to other people and ask for advice. If we are in the midst of puzzlement, we can read a book or consult others who have experienced the same situation. Eventually, we can make some choices, knowing that God is a God who has no problem if we make the wrong choice, who has no problem if we think we'd better think it out again and then make a different choice, until we finally get it right.

Scriptural Perspectives on Counsel

The words quoted on page 33 from the Letter to the Ephesians announce that God "accomplishes all things according to his counsel and will." Wonder of wonders. These words steep us in the wonder of God's activity in our lives. They tell us that the gift of counsel is not merely a little mysterious something, a tiny skill of some kind, that God gives us to help us muddle through. Rather, counsel is God active in us "accomplishing all things." If we can imagine. If we can.

Another perspective on the gift of counsel appears in the longer scriptural passage quoted on pages 33–34 from Revelation. There, counsel is precisely "the Spirit" giving guidance and pointing the way. The gift of counsel is the Spirit reminding us that no matter how secure or self-sufficient we think we are, no matter how little we may think we need, no matter how clearly we may think we see, we are deluding ourselves. We can be truly rich only in the things of the Spirit; we can be secure only through complete dependence on God; we can see only if we blink away the false vision, the phony point of view, and the superficial values of "the world," that is, the dominant culture insofar as it turns away from God and from truth in all its forms.

Toward the end of this passage from Revelation, with no prior notice, the speaker clearly seems to shift from the Spirit to the risen Christ: "Listen! I am standing at the door, knocking; if you hear my voice and open the door, I will come in to you and eat with you, and you with me. To the one who conquers I will give a place with me on my throne, just as I myself conquered and sat down with my Father on his throne" (3:20–21).

Only the risen Lord would speak of "my Father." It seems that there is some identification between the Spirit and the risen Christ. Indeed, the Holy Spirit is precisely the Spirit of the Lord—or, rather, the Spirit of the love shared by the Father and the Son, a Spirit that is both one with Father and Son and a distinct personal presence in the Trinity. So when we speak of the Holy Spirit's gift of counsel, we can be talking only about the gift that leads us along the path of Christ, in the love of the Father. The gift of counsel is the gift of the Holy Spirit that sheds the light of Christ in particular situations.

Indeed, if we had to sum up the gift of counsel in one brief sentence, we could say this: counsel helps us in particular sets of circumstances to distinguish what is real from what is unreal and to choose the real. "The real" may be a particular course of action, or it may be a particular goal, but counsel helps us see with eyes of faith, from God's point of view.

Has the drift of the discussion moved in a direction that is altogether too abstract and removed from real, everyday life? Perhaps. But perhaps we can anchor our discussion by consulting some of the deepest sources of wisdom available to us, namely, books purportedly written for children. There we can find some of the profoundest truths stated in language so simple even a grown-up can understand. Our "method," as theologians like to say, will be simple, unlike the methods cherished by many scholars. Let's see what this simple method may teach us about the gift of counsel.

Madeline

She was not afraid of mice—she loved winter, snow, and ice. To the tiger in the zoo Madeline just said, "Pooh-pooh."

Ludwig Bemelmans, *Madeline* (1939)[5]

Probably the heart of the matter, when it comes to the gift of counsel, not to mention the Christian life as a whole, is the need to do something about our fear. Almost any situation of any consequence in which we find ourselves is likely to scare the living daylights out of us, if we allow it to. To be open to whatever the gift of counsel may show us, in a particular situation, we are well advised to follow the example of Madeline.

A common-sense person, Madeline can see that the tiger is in a cage, so why should she be afraid? She just says, "Pooh-pooh." So should we to whatever gives us fear. Because of our faith, Christ has placed the source of all our fears in a securely locked cage. Christ tells us that fear is useless, that only trust has any use. In any particular situation that calls for trust, the gift of counsel whispers, "Relax! Trust! Do not be afraid! Just say, 'Pooh-pooh.'"

Once we listen to counsel regarding our fears, then we can listen to whatever this gift may offer in terms of specific suggestions for ways to act and steps to take.

Peter Pan

"Wendy, Wendy, when you are sleeping in your silly bed you might be flying about with me saying funny things to the stars."

J. M. Barrie, *Peter Pan* (1911)[6]

Counsel does not offer just sobersided advice against being afraid. Rather, it is a gift that invites us to go on the most amazing adventures sometimes. The life of Christian faith is a life of safety and security only in an ultimate sense, not in immediate, this-worldly terms; and the suggestions that come from the gift of counsel are sometimes suggestions to leave the safety of our silly beds and go flying about among the stars. Sometimes counsel beckons us to act in ways that may seem outrageous. Now this does not mean that if we choose to act in an outrageous fashion that we can blame our behavior on the Holy Spirit. It simply means that sometimes a responsible process of discernment may lead us to make a choice we would, perhaps earlier in life, have thought the wildest and craziest notion.

Peter Pan does not invite Wendy to become a mere eccentric. Instead, he invites her to fly. Metaphorically speaking, it is not altogether unlikely that, if we allow ourselves to listen to the gift of counsel, we could end up flying, as well. We could end up going places and doing things we might never otherwise have done. We could end up making choices that seem, on the face of it, to be imprudent in the extreme. We could end up acting in ways that seem outrageous to "respectable" people. We could even end up breaking some rules! When we open ourselves to the gift of counsel, anything, but anything, can happen. Even an adventure or two.

Winnie-the-Pooh

"I am a Bear of Very Little Brain, and long words Bother me."

A. A. Milne, *Winnie-the-Pooh* (1926)[7]

It may sometimes seem that the gift of counsel must lead to considerable pondering. At length, even. It may even seem to require us to become deep thinkers, if not amateur theologians. *Au contraire.* Counsel does not lead to elephantiasis of the intellect, and there is no need to develop profound theories to support the choices we end up making. If anything, counsel increases our ability to think simply. Even if one *already is* a theologian. In the life of faith, counsel helps us follow the famous nineteenth-century dictum of Henry David Thoreau, "Simplify, simplify...."[8]

The Christian life is not a life of anti-intellectualism or even of simplemindedness. But it is a life of simplicity in all respects. Unless one is a theologian, however, there is a very real sense in which long words should bother us. Counsel helps us think clearly and simply when we need to figure out where the Spirit is leading. We can, and should, be perfectly comfortable with that. For when it comes to the human mind compared to the mind of God, everyone is "a Bear of Very Little Brain."

Further Tales of Mr. Pengachoosa

"People nearly always know the right answers. They just like someone else to tell them."

Caroline Rush,
Further Tales of Mr. Pengachoosa (1967)[9]

It can be easy to take the gift of counsel for granted. It can seem like no gift at all, like a purely natural ability. We may be inclined to think we're required to put in many hours with furrowed brow, puzzling, puzzling, puzzling it out, and if it comes rather easily, what one should do in this particular situation, well, we may think that it cannot possibly be the right thing to do, because (a) we thought of it ourselves, (b) it required no anguish, and (c) everyone knows, "no pain, no gain." Once again, *au contraire.*

There are plenty of times when the gift of counsel will help us see the right path just like that. Simple as pie. Sometimes we will feel the nudge of the Spirit's elbow in our ribs almost immediately, and that's no problem. If it *seems* right, and the other people we consult think it is right, most of the time it *is* right. Don't overlook the consultation step, however. It means a great deal if someone else agrees with us about the right thing to do. The Holy Spirit is at the other person's elbow, too.

The Wizard of Oz

The Princess looked at her more closely.

"Tell me," she resumed, "are you of royal blood?"

"Better than that, ma'am," said Dorothy. "I came from Kansas."

L. Frank Baum, *The Wizard of Oz* (1900)[10]

One of the great benefits of the gift of counsel is its power to show us the spectacular holiness of the ordinary, not just in general, but in particular situations and circumstances. Take one of the most common examples. The setting is the bedroom of a sleeping infant or child. The father or mother stands by the child's bedside watching him or her, touched deeply by the sight. It is only natural for a mother or father to be filled with feelings of love in this situation. With counsel, however, the parent feels not only love but gratitude, and a gratitude that expresses itself prayerfully.

Here is what I mean. Given the gift of counsel, the watching father or mother knows that the sleeping infant is not just his or her child but a child of God. The child may look ordinary enough, like countless other children asleep in their beds, but counsel tells the parent that this ordinary-looking child, precisely *because* he or she is ordinary, is also holy, is also sacred. To use L. Frank Baum's images, this baby or toddler is the greatest thing of all because he or she is "from Kansas." Because God is the creator of all that is ordinary, and the ordinary echoes God's love constantly.

More than this, however, the parent watching the sleeping child has, by means of counsel, a personal experience of the mystery at the heart of the Incarnation itself. Counsel enables the parent to leap from the ordinary to the sacred in the blink of an eye. At such a moment it takes little effort to believe that the Son of God could come into the world as a perfectly human infant.

Of course, the gift of counsel sheds light in many more situations than this one, helping us recognize that "Kansas" is a symbol for the ordinary all around us—is holy precisely *because* it is "Kansas."

The Voyages of Doctor Doolittle

Great decisions often take no more than a moment
in the making.

Hugh Lofting,
The Voyages of Doctor Doolittle (1922)[11]

We tend to think that momentous decisions always require
a tortuous process of discernment. Otherwise, we think, the
decision must not be especially significant. Sometimes, it's
true, we arrive at important decisions—the choice of a life
vocation, for example—only after an extended decision-
making process. Such decisions are not ones that a person
should make lightly. On the other hand, there are people
for whom there simply was no doubt that they wanted
with all their heart to enter the religious life, or become a
fire fighter, or raise horses, for example. The case of Saint
Thérèse of Lisieux (1873–97), who knew for certain at the
age of fifteen that she wanted to become a Carmelite nun,
is not as exceptional a case as one might think.[12]

Sometimes the gift of counsel works this way, helping a
person to know without a long, involved process of discernment that a particular choice is right for him or her. Some
people know from childhood exactly what they want to do.
Popular children's author and illustrator Tomie de Paola,
for example, knew at a very young age that he wanted to
draw pictures for children's books.[13]

Of course, even people who make some "great decisions" in a moment's time find that they cannot make all
decisions this way. Counsel more commonly involves a
gradual leading toward a choice rather than a sudden insight
into the right direction to go.

The Little Prince

"Grown-ups never understand anything by themselves, and it is tiresome for children to be always and forever explaining things to them."

Antoine de Saint-Exupéry,
The Little Prince (1943)[14]

A life rooted in the spirit of the gospel is a life that is sometimes a source of great perplexity, and never more so than when it leads us to decisions the world is sure to view as unrealistic. One of the most common characteristics of gospel-inspired choices is that they strike others as being unrealistic in the extreme. All this means is that in people who follow such choices, the gift of counsel is so strong that it leads them to follow in a powerful way the words of Jesus: "Truly I tell you, whoever does not receive the kingdom of God as a little child will never enter it" (Mark 10:15).

Sometimes—more often than we are willing to listen, if the truth be told—counsel leads us to act as a child might naturally act, to see things as a child sees them. The world will insist that, for example, the ultimate form of security is money, including investments, insurance policies, and so forth. Meanwhile, a child has no conception of the need for money but trusts implicitly in his or her parents' providence. Just as the gospel quietly insists that we place ourselves in the hands of divine Providence.

Financial forms of security are fine, but there is such a thing as too much dependence on money. There needs to be a point at which we say, "Whoa!" Some ways to limit our emotional dependence on money include simply giving it away to those who need it more than we do, contributing to the good works of the Church, or simply supporting our parishes.

The main point, however, is that counsel often leads us to act as a child might act, to look at life and the world as a child does. Instead of giving ourselves over entirely to a jaded, "realistic," "adult" way of thinking and acting at all times and in all places, to give up our adult solemnities and embrace the playful ways of a child.

Opposites

What is the opposite of *two?*
A lonely me, a lonely you.

Richard Wilbur, *Opposites* (1973)[15]

There is something in popular forms of Roman Catholic spirituality that turns a healthy inclination toward solitude into an unhealthy preference for individualism. Counsel insists that prayerful solitude is vital to a healthy, balanced faith life. We need to have times "alone with God." Otherwise, we are likely to give ourselves up to the "herd mentality" that governs so much of modern life, allowing the dominant culture to tell us what to wear, how to look, what to eat, and what to buy that we really don't need. Without times for prayerful solitude we begin to forget that a gospel life is bound to be a countercultural life. Counsel speaks of this consistently.

At the same time, counsel reminds us that a Christian life is a life in community. The Eucharist, the "source and summit" of the Christian life, is a *communal* ritual. Even when we are in prayerful solitude, we are a member of the spiritual community of the Church. There is no "Jesus and me off in a corner by ourselves" dimension to a Christian life. This communal character is far from superficial, however. It is a deep reality, and sometimes it is best served when a faith community is together in silence.

Sometimes, counsel reminds us, superficial communal interactions can actually short-circuit the deeper communal dimension of the Christian life. Consider, for example, liturgical situations in which a priest, music minister, or lector gives us virtually no choice but to introduce ourselves to the folks in the next pew, hold hands during the Our Father, or hug people we haven't even been introduced to. Such "instant intimacy," in my view, is a poor substitute for an authentic, prayerful experience of spiritual community that can happen only, paradoxically, when everyone respects each one's solitude as the congregation together turns toward the risen Christ present in its midst.

The Enchanted Forest

Let us not worry about the future. Those who do what is right are always rewarded.

Bernice Schenk de Regniers,
The Enchanted Forest (1974)[16]

One of the gospel messages we find most difficult to hear and take to heart is the admonition repeated often by Jesus to stop worrying about the future:

Therefore do not worry, saying, "What will we eat?" or "What will we drink?" or "What will we wear?" For it is the Gentiles who strive for all these things; and indeed your heavenly Father knows that you need all these things. But strive first for the kingdom of God and his righteousness, and all these things will be given to you as well. So do not worry about tomorrow, for tomorrow will bring worries of its own. Today's trouble is enough for today (Matthew 6:31–34).

The Holy Spirit's gift of counsel reminds us that faith would have us trust instead of being anxiety ridden. Counsel places all things in the ultimate context of God's love. If we believe—if we actually *know*—that God loves us, what is there to worry about? Even if five minutes from now one were to be executed for a crime one did not commit, there is no need for worry. Our ultimate destiny is not in time and space. Regardless of when our mortal ends arrive, we are made for bigger and better things, glorious and good though this life certainly is. So, the gift of counsel says, do not worry. Only try to do what is right today in all our doings big and small, and let tomorrow take care of itself.

Instead, we are among the biggest "worrywarts" the world has ever known, and many of our biggest worries have to do with money. Will we have enough money? Where will we get it? How will we pay next month's mortgage? How will we buy warm enough clothes for our children? More often than not, counsel advises us to stop looking ahead with fear. Instead, look back and take heart. Was there ever a time when, in the long run, God was not there in the thick of things, bringing all things to good for those who love God? When our fear about "what might happen" is greatest, the gift of counsel whispers insistently to look back and take heart.

CHAPTER FOUR

The Gift of Fortitude

O f all the gifts of the Holy Spirit, the gift of fortitude is the one that is most commonly thought of and, frequently, the most underappreciated—especially in ourselves. In fact, fortitude is also one of the cardinal virtues. In this case, a gift is also a virtue. The gift of fortitude is the capacity to remain "firm in hope against all pressures, even death."[1] When fidelity to the gospel brings suffering, desolation of spirit, or the need to tolerate controversy, the gift of fortitude helps us not to give in to fear. It also helps us not to act in a self-righteous or egotistical manner, or to be destructive about the ways we show fortitude.

Fortitude Helps Us Confront Cultural Trends

One difficulty, when it comes to a gift that is also a virtue, is that we may easily overlook its presence through false humility. Look at it this way. Another word for fortitude is courage, and if we use this word, perhaps it becomes more clear how fortitude is a gift, not something that comes naturally. More than likely, we live in a courageous manner just about every day and fail to take much notice of it. We could talk about some obvious examples of courage, life-and-death situations in which we might risk life for the faith, or stand-up-for-social-justice situations in which we risk being tossed in the slammer. These are all fine, and we need to give credit where it's due. But to better reflect on fortitude in our eve- ryday experiences, we shall look, instead, for some everyday examples of how people live the gift of fortitude, or courage.

First, we might think about the ways people act with courage in the face of silly cultural trends. Choose one at random. Say the cosmetic-surgery trend. To be more specific, how about the liposuction trend? To paraphrase the late, great Chicago newspaper columnist Mike Royko, who hit the nail on the head: "Anyone who gives a surgeon six thousand dollars for vacuuming fat out of one's body should give some thought to investing a little more in adding cells to the brain."[2]

It takes fortitude, sometimes, for people to dismiss as silly the idea that there is something wrong with the wrinkles in their faces or the bulges in their figures. Of course, a great many people couldn't afford the price of plastic surgery even if they wanted it. But the point is that it takes courage not to let a cultural trend erode one's sense of personal dignity, not to let one's self-esteem depend on what the culture says about what's attractive and what's not.

Another cultural trend that seems to have staying power is the celebration of youthful looks and the embarrassment at the natural signs of human aging. Got gray hair? Dye it! Got facial wrinkles and sags? Buy out the cosmetics coun- ter! The examples are numerous, of course, but the gift of fortitude helps us accept ourselves as we age. It's perfectly okay to be an old person! Cosmetics and surgery may alter some of the surface signs of aging—temporarily—but that is all. Fortitude helps us rely more on common sense. Got money you can afford to spend on a nose job? If so, perhaps it might be better to give it to your favorite charity, instead.

Unless one's nose is malfunctioning, it's fine. It's who we are and how we live our lives that matter, that make us beautiful or not.

Of course, there are a great many more cultural trends that test the gift of fortitude. Often, these appear in the form of subtle or not-so-subtle peer pressures, and not infrequently in the dominant culture, mass-market advertising plays a key role. If we stop to think about it, the extent to which the advertising industry influences our behavior can be downright frightening. Indeed, if advertising once had the primary function of informing people about products and services designed to meet actual human needs, today advertising frequently functions to *create* needs we didn't know we had. When this happens, fortitude helps us recognize an artificial "need" for what it is and respond accordingly.

One of the earliest examples of the advertising industry's creating a need for products we didn't know we needed is breath fresheners. Prior to the post-World War II years, there was virtually no market for mouthwashes and other related products. Once the advertising industry did its job, however—and this is when television began to show its enormous advertising power—people began to realize how badly their breath smelled, and the market for breath fresheners grew enormously. Today, few self-respecting persons would go out into the world in the morning without first making sure that their breath was absolutely fresh. Thank you, Madison Avenue! Breath fresheners have gone way beyond being a mere product to being a part of the dominant culture itself, a part the first half of the twentieth century didn't even know existed.

When this happens, when a product becomes a part of the dominant culture, fortitude probably becomes irrelevant, since this cultural pressure short-circuits the moral dimension.

What's worse, advertising can pressure us in negative ways that can affect our health. Take, for instance, the promotion of food products that are virtually nutrition free. Fortitude can help us recognize glitzy convenience foods that have no nutritional value.

Fortitude Integrates the Spirit and the Body

But what, you may ask, does this have to do with our faith? Such a question reveals a common misunderstanding of spirituality in our time, one that regards body and soul as only accidentally related. This dualistic view of human nature is as old as the hills, going back even to before Christianity, to the cultures of ancient Greece and Rome. Body/soul dualism infected Christianity early in its history, to be sure. But it is more faithful to Christianity's Jewish roots to recover the ancient Israelite conviction that body and soul are one and cannot be separated.

Thus, anything that affects the body also affects the soul, and vice versa. So our eating habits are not just a physical issue; they are a spiritual issue, too. To tank up on empty calories is to deprive the soul of the nutrition it needs to live fully, and breathe, and have its being in Christ. Fortitude helps us resist mass-market advertising's pressure to buy and consume foods that are little more than white flour, sugar, and, not infrequently, fat.

Fortitude Helps Us Embrace Our Sexuality in Healthy Ways

Another way the gift of fortitude can affect our everyday living is in our feelings about and attitudes toward sexuality.

Essentially, human sexuality is relational, the innate capacity to relate to others in warm, caring ways.[3] Fortitude helps us live as sexual beings, regardless of our vocations. For married couples, it is appropriate for their sexual love for each other to have a genital expression. For people who are not married, a genital expression is *not* appropriate. For both married and unmarried people, however, being comfortable with their and others' sexuality is a basic component of spirituality. For the ability to show a warm, caring love for one another depends on our ability to be comfortable with ourselves. Fortitude helps married couples have a healthy genital-sexual love. It also helps unmarried people express love in healthy non-genital-sexual ways.

Lest we trivialize what we are saying, we need to keep in mind that both married and unmarried people need *discipline* when it comes to the integration of sexuality into one's vocation.

Fortitude can be a considerable blessing, helping married couples understand and live according to the truth that "sexual lovemaking is one of the most difficult of the spir- itual arts."[4] Yes, making love comes naturally to us. We have a natural and spiritual drive toward genital union. At the same time, making love is an art that a married couple must learn, and fortitude helps the couple to keep learning this art over the many years of a marriage. In fact, there is more to this than may be apparent.

During the early months and years of a marriage, husband and wife need to learn about each other's sexual rhythms and, through generosity, sensitivity, and compromise, to learn to integrate sexual lovemaking into their marriage, and into their role as parents, if they have children, in ways that "work" for them. Fortitude helps a couple to be both persistent and patient, knowing that sexual lovemaking is not peripheral but basic to marital spirituality. And as a marriage moves into the middle years, as the children grow up and leave for lives of their own, fortitude helps husband and wife not to let sexual lovemaking become less important.

All along the way, throughout the years of a marriage, fortitude helps spouses seek not just each one's own pleasure but a true "making of love" that comes from shared pleasure. It takes fortitude to give each other sexual pleasure and to see, paradoxically, that one's pleasure comes from, and is increased by, giving one's spouse pleasure. And right about now, gentle reader, you may find yourself at least a little bit uncomfortable with all this talk of "pleasure" and its importance in a book on the gifts of the Holy Spirit. Here is dualism raising its head again. We often find it difficult, if not impossible, to believe that "something as earthy, as passionate, as irrational and biological as sexual activity could incarnate God's loving presence. Yet that is precisely what the sexual experience of two millennia of Christians reveals."5

Fortitude helps us, if we are married, not to turn away from sexual pleasure out of an inappropriate guilt dwelling in the deep, dark recesses of the unconscious mind and grounded in a body/soul dualism completely incompatible with authentic Christianity and its Jewish roots. Rather, fortitude gives us the courage to welcome and give sexual pleasure while turning a deaf ear to any echoes of Puritan dualism. Fortitude helps us ignore any interpretations of Christianity that, out of fear, overspiritualize faith.

Fortitude Helps Us Overcome All Our Fears

Of course, there are many other examples of the ways that fortitude helps us transcend fear and become more loving people. It helps us face the fear of intimacy, in general. When a conflict needs to be resolved, fortitude helps us face it rather than run the other way. When we are reluctant to show love, fortitude can be the spiritual spark plug that moves us to buy a rose or give a hug, give the gift of time to pursue a hobby or special interest, or leave a love note where our beloved will find it later.

Parents, too, know the power of fortitude when being a mother or father requires the courage to say no and keep on saying no. Fortitude gives parents the staying power to hang in there with a child who fails to meet parental expectations of whatever kind. Each stage of parenthood brings its own rewards and challenges, fulfillments and disappointments. Relatively few parents are lucky enough to have kids who all through adolescence and young adulthood live up to their parents' ideals and expectations.

When the infant needs to learn that bedtime is bedtime, and that's the end of the discussion, fortitude helps parents let the baby cry himself or herself to sleep for a couple of evenings, until the baby gets the message that crying won't delay bedtime. When the two-year-old begins to exercise his or her power to say "No!" fortitude helps parents respond in appropriate ways, perhaps by giving the child choices instead of turning the situation into a power struggle.

When a teenager makes choices of which both parents and society disapprove, fortitude helps parents to be companions to the adolescent as he or she lives with, and through, the consequences. The gift of fortitude helps parents to let the teenager know that he or she is loved without trying to intervene to save the kid from the consequences of his or her actions.

Fortitude Is a Gift for the Real World

The point is simply that fortitude is not an abstraction or a mere theological theory. Rather, fortitude—like all seven of the gifts of the Holy Spirit—is a gift meant for the real, everyday world and the lives of real, everyday people. Fortitude is a gift we can expect from our ongoing intimacy with the risen Christ. It is a gift we can pray for, asking the Holy Spirit for an increase of this gift at times when we feel a need for courage in the face of all kinds of ordinary situations. Fortitude is for the real situations in our real relationships in the real world. So we shouldn't be shy about praying for this gift when we feel we need it the most. For when we ask, we will discover that we already have what we've been praying for.

We need fortitude not just in our everyday relationships, however. There are times in every life when fortitude is necessary if truth and fairness are not to be buried by lies and injustice. These are situations in which ordinary people are called to stand up for what is right, however insignificant the situation may seem or however minor the issues involved.

One of the most common settings that calls for heroic fortitude in unspectacular ways is the workplace. Quite often, people give not a second thought when it comes to taking advantage of their employers. We may fudge a little—in our favor, of course—on the time sheet, thus reporting that we worked a little longer than we actually did. We may need some pencils at home, so we pocket a few from the office. The computer at work has access to the Internet, so we may spend time "surfing the Net" when we should be working. Or we may use the copy machine for personal purposes without reimbursing our employers. Fortitude helps us resist the inclination to do such things, even when "everyone is doing it." Of course, things can work the other way, too.

True story: A man worked in a large neighborhood grocery store, one that had to struggle constantly to compete with the big chain supermarkets in town. Twice thieves broke into the store at night and stole merchandise. Finally, the man decided to park his car across the street from the back of the store and stay there all night to see if he could catch the burglars. The grocery store did not belong to him, but he wanted to do all he could to help the store remain in business. So after the store closed late in the evening, the man went home, sat down to dinner with his family, then returned to keep watch until 4:00 A.M., when he would head home for a few hours of sleep before going to work again. On the third night of his vigil, the man's efforts paid off.

About 2:30 A.M., a truck pulled up to the back of the grocery store. Two men got out and began to break into the rear entrance, just as they had on the two previous occasions. Watching from his car across the street and down the block, the faithful employee called the police on his cellular phone. They arrived in a few minutes and caught the burglars in the act.

The next day, the owner of the grocery store told newspaper and television reporters that he was grateful to his employee for taking personal action to stop his store from being broken into. He said he was inspired that his employee cared enough to keep watch for the thieves on his own time. Finally, he said that the man was not just his employee but his friend, and for that he was deeply thankful.6

This is yet another example of how fortitude can come into play in everyday situations. The grocery store employee had the courage to sacrifice his own time to help his employer and his employer's business. With fortitude, he did something no one expected him to do because it was the right thing to do.

Most of the ways that fortitude helps us live the spirit of the gospel are unspectacular. Of course, Martin Luther King, Jr., needed fortitude to lead the civil-rights movement of the 1960s, Nelson Mandela needed this gift to inspire opposition to apartheid in South Africa, Dorothy Day needed fortitude to co-found and lead the Catholic Worker movement in the United States from 1932 until her death in 1980, and Saint Thérèse of Lisieux needed heroic fortitude to make of an obscure life in an obscure nineteenth-century French convent a life of heroic holiness that inspires people down to our own time. But as the examples we have discussed so far illustrate, for most of us the gift of fortitude comes into play in the most everyday, unnoticeable circumstances.

Fortitude Keeps Us Faithful to Our Vision

There is a unique way that the gift of fortitude becomes active in some people's lives yet remains unnoticed by virtually everyone. Writers, musicians, and artists of all kinds need fortitude if they are to be faithful to the unique vision each one has. The temptation for an artist to produce work that will "sell" can be powerful, indeed. If an artist, writer, or musician is to be faithful to his or her unique gifts, however, he or she must be willing to "go out on a limb" and, sometimes, even jump off into what looks like sheer space with no safety net below. Fear of general disapproval, fear of scorn, can be great. Still, fortitude has made possible the priceless works of genius known and treasured the world over.

Fortitude made it possible in the eighteenth century for Wolfgang Amadeus Mozart to write his ground-breaking opera *The Magic Flute,* and it made it possible for him to continue working on his *Requiem,* even during his last illness. Although scholars frequently overlook Mozart's

Catholicism, thus dismissing its importance as a source of inspiration for his music, Mozart's Roman Catholic faith had a profound impact on his life and music, and fortitude had much to do with how faithful he was to his inner vision, right up until his death at the age of thirty-one.[7]

Were it not for fortitude, in the nineteenth century Vincent van Gogh would not have produced his famous paintings *Sunflowers* and *Starry Night,* which reflect the sacred in creation in almost shocking terms. The same may be said of less well-known yet equally revelatory works such as *The Potato Eaters* and *Girl Kneeling in Front of a Cradle.* The former shows the poverty and dignity of peasant people in van Gogh's time. He wrote: "Such pictures may teach [us] something."[8] The latter reveals van Gogh's conviction that God is present in the most ordinary settings. He wrote that "if one feels the need of something grand, something infinite, something that makes one feel aware of God, one need not go far to find it. I think I see something deeper, more infinite, more eternal than the ocean in the expression of the eyes of a little baby when it wakes in the morning, and coos or laughs because it sees the sun shining on its cradle...."[9]

In the twentieth century, Catholic writer Flannery O'Connor (1925–64) wrote stories that were astonishing in their portrayal of characters and situations that were anything but conventional. In the words of theologian Walter J. Burghardt, S.J., "Many reviewers have been baffled by Flannery's stories, mainly because they center on the operations of grace in the lives of very natural men and women."[10]

O'Connor's Southern fundamentalist Christians, her brash unbelievers, her crazy traveling Bible salesman, and her pitiful grandmother who is killed by an escaped convict, all serve her purpose to write stories about authentic and inauthentic faith and the presence of grace in the most unlikely circumstances. Hazel Motes, the central character in O'Connor's best-known story, "Wise Blood," refuses to have anything to do with anything less than God, and that includes religion. O'Connor could not have written such stories without the gift of fortitude.

Not only was O'Connor a gifted writer of fiction but she wrote hundreds of letters, published posthumously, that reveal she was no slouch when it came to spiritual insight. In one letter, written to a young college student named Alfred Corn, she addressed his declaration that he had lost his faith:

> I think that this experience you are having of losing your faith, or as you think, of having lost it, is an experience that in the long run belongs to faith; or at least it can belong to faith if faith is still valuable to you, and it must be or you would not have written me about this.
>
> I don't know how the kind of faith required of a Christian living in the 20th century can be at all if it is not grounded on this experience that you are having right now of unbelief....[11]

In both her stories and her letters, O'Connor relied on fortitude to help her present belief and unbelief as two sides of the same coin. It takes courage to say to the world that faith is authentic only when it purifies itself by refusing to believe anything except the truth. It takes fortitude to say this in a world in which the faith of many sincerely religious people is, in part at least, unintentionally idolatrous. Many well-meaning people worship not God but limited ideas of God; not God but doctrines; not God but rituals; not God but religious institutions. O'Connor had the courage to write stories and letters proclaiming that while many things less than God can help us to God, ultimately only God is worthy of the human heart.

O'Connor's writing was never without wit, and she allowed this to surface even more explicitly, from time to time, when she wrote book reviews. She knew a poorly written book when she saw one, and she was not afraid to say so, but not without a twinkle in her eye. For example, in a 1960 review of a biography of Francis Cardinal Spellman, the archbishop of New York, O'Connor wrote: "Cardinal Spellman has apparently often given as many as seven talks a day, a feat which would kill a lesser man, but which must account for the ease with which he exercises the clerical gift for bringing forth the sonorous familiar phrase of slowly deadening effect."12

Lest we take such a remark too lightly, keep in mind that—especially during this period of U.S. Catholic history—it took more than a little courage for O'Connor to write in such a vein about one of the most prominent Roman Catholic leaders of the time. The gift of fortitude was definitely active here.

Another twentieth-century Roman Catholic author who relied heavily on fortitude was the novelist Graham Greene (1904–91). In his modern classic *The Heart of the Matter*, for example, Scobie, the central character of the story, takes his own life. As the narrative draws to a close, Scobie's wife consults the priest Father Rank, convinced that her husband has condemned himself to hell for all eternity for committing suicide—a common Roman Catholic belief prior to the Second Vatican Council in the mid-1960s. Father Rank responds impatiently:

> "For goodness' sake, Mrs. Scobie, don't imagine you or I know a thing about God's mercy."
>
> "The Church says..."
>
> "I know the Church says. The Church knows all the rules. But it doesn't know what goes on in a single human heart."13

We live in an era when these words do not seem shocking at all, but when *The Heart of the Matter* was first published, in 1948, the times were altogether different. It took a healthy dose of fortitude for Greene to write words that clashed so clearly with the official Roman Catholic teaching of the time. Not only did Greene have one of his characters, a priest, disagree with that teaching, but he had the character do so at a time when no "good Catholic" would disagree with "the Church" so publicly.

Fortitude Animates an Authentic Life of Faith

Fortitude helps us live lives of authentic faith. Indeed, without fortitude, faith comes close to being impossible. At the same time, part of any life of faith is the need to live in the light of one's own mortality—and "light" is precisely what we find when we embrace the fact that our days and hours on this earth are limited. Words from "Long Train of Dreams" by singer/songwriter John Stewart are true for us all: "I am a traveler, / I am riding through time. / I have a ticket to the end of the line."14

Each one of us is "a traveler," and the end of our line *will* come. It takes fortitude to accept the truth of our own mortality and then live each day not morbidly but joyfully. That our ultimate destiny is beyond this time and space should not fill us with terror. Rather, it is a truth by which God means to liberate us.

For the gift of fortitude may easily enable us to imagine God speaking to us, both now and at the instant of death, some other words from Stewart's song: "I'll hold you forever at the end of the line."15

CHAPTER FIVE

The Gift of Knowledge

Atlanta, Georgia: July, 1998
A man who was practicing banjo on his back porch
heard some strange noises from his peach orchard
and interrupted his practicing to see what the com-
motion was. Still having his banjo strapped to him
and believing it was a wild boar that commonly
got drunk from eating falling fermented peaches,
he rushed into the peach orchard. "As I entered the
orchard, I saw strange lights and heard a strange
humming noise. Suddenly, I was struck dumb and
paralyzed by some kind of light beam," said Delmore
Frichter, lead banjoist and publicist of the Sheepmas-
ters bluegrass band. "I felt myself being sucked up
into the air just before I lost consciousness.

"The next thing I remember was being strapped
down on a table in sort of a misty interior with some
kind of a flood light in my face. Right there, strapped
down on a table next to me, was my prized Gibson
prewar Granada! They were doing horrible things to
my banjo! They were inserting probes and stuff into
the resonator flange holes. They had almond shaped
eyes, no ears and their skins were grayish with a shiny
texture just like duct tape!"

Frichter, who is now in deep regression therapy, also stated that other than this brief remembrance, he later found himself lying on the ground of his orchard and was awakened by "that damned drunken boar" named "Norman" nibbling at his toes. He further states that he lost as much as five hours by his own estimate because when he staggered back into the house he compared his wall clock to his watch which had stopped.

"They took my Granada! I think they thought it was some kind of secret device or something. If I ever get my hands on those thieving frogs, they'll have faces full of buckshot!" exclaimed Frichter.

The insurance company that covers household loss refused to reimburse the banjoist the $15,000 of claimed value of the missing banjo stating that the circumstances surrounding the incident were suspicious and until Frichter's story can be verified, such a loss was not covered under his current policy. "Life isn't always a bowl of chili," Frichter stated.[1]

What, you may wonder, does a spoof such as this have to do with the Holy Spirit's gift of knowledge? First, the account of banjoist Delmore Frichter's adventure with space aliens illustrates a common misunderstanding when it comes to faith. People often think that faith is supposed to give us a form of knowledge unavailable to those without faith, just as Frichter claims that he has knowledge those never carried off by space aliens do not have.

Second, Frichter acts as if there were nothing unbelievable about his adventure. He simply reports what happened, and he expects everyone to take his words at face value. But in fact, everyone who hears the account is going to think ol' Delmore no longer has both oars in the water. In a sense, the gift of knowledge that comes from the Holy Spirit might seem to be similar to the "knowledge" Delmore has. For each of us has knowledge of realities we will never be able to prove to anyone who lives with a perspective other than that of faith, or whose understanding of faith is incompatible with the Roman Catholic view.

Knowledge Is Insight

The gift of knowledge is nothing like that. Knowledge helps us comprehend divine truths even when, ultimately, the human mind cannot completely grasp them.[2] This comprehension is based not on a complete shut down of the intellect but on the admission that it can go only so far. To acknowledge the limits of the intellect does not mean that we embrace the nonsense of "blind faith." It simply means that we are able to admit the overwhelming greatness of God.

Another way to put this is to say that *knowledge* is very much like *insight*. Here is what a dictionary says about *insight*:

1. The capacity to discern the true nature of a situation; penetration.
2. The act or outcome of grasping the inward or hidden nature of things or of perceiving in an intuitive manner.[3]

So the gift of knowledge does not mean that we have the capacity for a precise, complete, scientific grasp of divine realities. If we had, we would be God. Rather, knowledge makes it possible for us to grasp the inner nature of things, to perceive in an intuitive manner without our being able to comprehend completely.

Take the sacraments, for example. A completely objective observer can be an uninvolved spectator when it
comes to the sacraments, and he or she can see everything
that happens without seeing what's really taking place. A
believer, on the other hand, is not a completely objective
observer and does not view the sacraments as an outsider.
A believer experiences the sacraments *from the inside,* with
insight—that is, from the perspective offered by the gift of
knowledge.

The gift of knowledge is nothing like the "knowledge"
gained by our old friend Frichter. Knowledge does not give us
"information" no one else has. Rather, it gives us a *perspective* or point of view, one that comes from the experience of
faith, of an intimate relationship with the risen Christ and
the Church.

One way to understand the gift of knowledge is to use the
analogy of a loving marriage. After years together, spouses
gain an insight into each other that they can talk about but
that they cannot fully explain to anyone else. Their trust,
their commitment to each other, their capacity for forgiveness, their physical intimacy that cannot be separated from
their spiritual intimacy, their shared sense of humor, the
simple, quiet comfort they get from being with each other—
all this and more gives them a "knowledge," an "insight"
that transcends the "one-plus-one-equals-two-ness" of their
relationship. Their marriage gives them a perspective on
life and the world unavailable from any other source. They
know, for example, that their love for each other gives them
a glimpse of the kingdom of heaven.

Knowledge Provides a "God's-Eye View" of the World

In a similar way, faith—loving intimacy with the risen Lord—gives those for whom faith is more than an opinion a special insight. This knowledge—in truth, we might well call it a kind of wisdom—is not complicated. It is a way of seeing all things in a certain light, the light of faith that puts all things in their proper perspective. A poem written by the late Mark Van Doren, titled "Slowly, Slowly Wisdom Gathers," explains the kind of knowledge we're talking about. From the gift of knowledge we begin to see how things are:

> *The web of the world, how thick, how thin,*
> *How firm, with all things folded in;*
> *How ancient, and how full of grace.*[4]

This is what the gift of knowledge is about—seeing how things really are, from a God's-eye point of view, no matter what we gaze upon, examine, or experience.

We shouldn't romanticize the gift of knowledge, however: it is not all about sweetness and light. *All* the world, *all* the universe, and *all* human experience come under the perspective of knowledge. Knowledge has as much to do with pain and anguish as it does with happiness and fulfillment.

A predominantly secular view of life and the world finds it difficult to discover any meaning in the dark side of human experience. This is why, for example, euthanasia, or "mercy killing," finds so many supporters today. From a purely secular perspective, it makes no sense for a person who is terminally ill to live with physical suffering for an indeterminate time when his or her suffering could be ended in some "humane" fashion. "Why not put him out of his misery?" the secular point of view asks. "Why not let her flip a switch to inject herself with drugs that will end her life and her suffering?"

The Holy Spirit's gift of knowledge helps us see, on the contrary, that we have no right to kill, either another or ourselves, regardless of the reason.5 When we suffer, we believe, we share in the suffering of Christ to whom we belong through our baptism. Just as Jesus' suffering has redemptive value, so our suffering, in Christ, has redemptive value. Only faith gifted with knowledge gives us this insight into the true nature of things.

Those who promote "mercy killing" do so because, they say, they believe in human dignity; they see a terminally ill life filled with pain as no longer worth living. On the contrary, says the gift of knowledge, even a life of pain is a life worth living. Euthanasia is an act of despair, pure and simple.

Some ten or twelve years before he died of natural causes, Roman Catholic fiction writer and essayist André Dubus stopped his car on a foggy night to help some people who had been in an automobile accident. Moments later, Dubus himself was struck by a passing car. He lost one leg and the use of the other. Some years later, Dubus wrote:

> Today is the twenty-ninth of August 1988, and since the twenty-third of June, the second of two days when I wanted to die, I have not wanted my earthly life to end, have not wanted to confront You [i.e., Christ] with anger and despair. I receive You in the Eucharist at daily Mass, and look at You on the cross, but mostly I watch the priest, and the old deacon, a widower, who brings me the Eucharist; and the people who walk past me to receive; and I know they have all endured their own agony, and prevailed in

their own way, though not alone but drawing their hope and strength from those they love, those who love them; and from You, in the sometimes tactile, sometimes incomprehensible, sometimes seemingly lethal way that You give.6

This is how it goes for those who live with the mysterious, provocative gift of knowledge, a gift that sometimes sheds light, sometimes seems only to deepen the darkness, but— wonder of wonders—sometimes brings insight all the same, even in the darkest night.

Knowledge Imparts Broad-Mindedness

When it comes to Roman Catholics, in particular, the gift of knowledge seems to impart insight also in the sense of *broad-mindedness*. Ideally, Catholics find the divine mystery in countless places and endless circumstances. We should find it difficult to limit God to "just here" or "just there." For us, God should be everywhere, with the sacred bursting out all over. Consider these words of Father Andrew Greeley about the Roman Catholic sense of the sacred:

Catholics live in an enchanted world, a world of statues and holy water, stained glass and votive candles, saints and religious medals, rosary beads and holy pictures. But these Catholic paraphernalia are mere hints of a deeper and more pervasive religious sensibility which inclines Catholics to see the Holy lurking in creation. As Catholics, we find our houses and our world haunted by a sense that the objects, events, and persons of daily life are revelations of divine grace.7

Knowledge tells us that God cannot be confined or limited to certain holy buildings, such as churches; certain officially sacred offices, such as the papacy; certain holy books, such as the Bible. Rather, churches, the papacy, and the Bible are holy—*can* be holy—because *holiness is everywhere.* Catholics should revel in the holiness of all things, for, as knowledge tells us, sin is not the most basic reality (the historical Protestant conviction); rather, grace is the most basic reality. For "where sin increased, grace abounded all the more..." (Romans 5:20b).

So we revel in votive candles, crucifixes, and holy pictures (even though some new parish churches make no room for them), and elaborate church interiors (even though there are some who want to give us sterile, Calvinistic worship halls). And we celebrate Mary, the mother of Jesus and our mother, too, who shows us the maternal love of God. We celebrate the saints of all eras because they show us the endless faces of God. We find the home to have a sacredness just as real as the sacredness of a church, each in its own way, because grace abounds and is not confined to certain places, ideas, persons, books, or doctrines.

The gift of knowledge helps us believe that grace is more powerful than sin. Catholicism believes humanity is first of all "saved," not "fallen"—though "fallen" it definitely is. We prefer to accentuate the positive while still taking the negative seriously.

Catholic broadness of mind embraces aspects of human nature and human experience that do not spring to mind first when we think of "the sacred." For Catholicism, the holy is precisely in the ordinary. For historical Protestantism, and for contemporary evangelical Protestant fundamentalism, sin is all around and the best bet is to be "saved," or rescued, from rampant sin—which, of course, Jesus will do if one "accepts him as your personal savior."

On the contrary, Catholics believe that what is all over the place is grace, not sin, abounding even in the most unlikely people, places, and events of daily life. For example, lively laughter over a funny event, an ordinary meal shared with ordinary people, a riotous day with babies and toddlers, a cup of hot chocolate on a winter's day, a patient hour with an apparently "lost" teenager or young adult—all are sacred. Sometimes the holy erupts when we least expect it.

Knowledge Enables Us to See God's Grace Abounding

In her delightful novel *Household Saints,* Francine Prose captures this sense of the enchanted nature of ordinary Catholic experience in the first sentences of her story:

> It happened by the grace of God that Joseph Santangelo won his wife in a card game. This fateful game of pinochle took place in the back room of Santangelo's Sausage Shop, on Mulberry Street, in New York City, on the last night of the record-breaking heat wave of September, 1949.8

How wild! How bizarre! That grace could happen in such circumstances. At the end of the story, like the other book-end, the novelist concludes by encouraging us to put away our unbelief, to be broad enough of mind to acknowledge that such things can, and do, happen:

> Wait. Such things can happen to anyone, on any hot night—a hot night exactly like this. Hush. Listen to the sound of cards slapping on the table. God is sending us a saint.9

This is how grace works, Prose reminds us, in the real, the ordinary, the mundane. The Holy Spirit gives knowledge, and suddenly, or gradually, we see that grace abounds. We see that the only thing that can fence grace in is narrowness of mind—and sometimes not even that.

Knowledge Reveals God's Presence Everywhere

The gift of knowledge is not, however, limited to a way of seeing. It is also the gift of a way to *perceive* all things. This is why a lively Catholic faith can stand on the top of a mountain or in the midst of a city's busy streets and perceive God's presence in both places. Knowledge reveals God present in virtually any set of circumstances. A mysticism of nature may embrace a redwood tree and declare that the divine Spirit is present in the tree, the forest, the star-filled skies at night, and faith can agree. But faith gifted with knowledge perceives God just as present in the home of any family. Knowledge can even find God in the anguish of parents at wit's end with their teenage children and in the frustration and anger of the teenagers themselves.

The gift of knowledge also helps us not to limit our perception of God's presence to what "the signs of the times" seem to indicate about the future, bringing us hope in the face of the most dire predictions. Probably no one has illustrated this Catholic capacity to keep our options open better than G. K. Chesterton. In his first novel, *The Napoleon of Notting Hill* (1904), Chesterton articulated his vision of the world as, above all, a place where God is at play:

> The human race, to which so many of my readers belong, has been playing at children's games from the beginning....And one of the games to which it

is most attached is called, "Keep to-morrow dark," and which is also named (by the rustics in Shropshire, I have no doubt) "Cheat the prophet." The players listen carefully and respectfully to all that the clever men have to say about what is to happen in the next generation. The players then wait until all the clever men are dead, and bury them nicely. They then go and do something else. That is all. For a race of simple tastes, however, it is great fun.

For human beings, being children, have the childish willfulness and the childish secrecy. And they never have from the beginning of the world done what the wise men have seen as inevitable. They stoned the false prophets, it is said; but they could have stoned true prophets with a greater and juster enjoyment.10

The gift of knowledge helps us see that all the prognostications about the future—of the Church and of the world—are little more than guessing games. No one is bound to do what the experts declare, and the world is not bound by any announcements of doom that come from the high towers of those who claim to see a future of ecological disaster or political chaos, for example. For the human heart is not bound by what prophets, true of false, may say.

At first glance, this may seem like little more than a Pollyanna outlook. Nothing, however, could be further from the truth. The world view that comes from knowledge is nothing if not realistic. Knowledge takes darkness and evil seriously. It is never surprised by human cruelty. But at the same time, it believes in the ultimate victory of good over evil.

In his novel *Mr. White's Confession,* Robert Clark tells a story about innocence and good intentions gone awry. The central character, Herbert White—a well-meaning but shy and socially inept young man—spends nearly twenty-eight years in prison for the murder of Ruby Fahey, a young woman he knew and cared for. Herbert is innocent of the crime, but through a series of misunderstandings and his own inability to remember, plus the misplaced zeal of a small-time police detective, he ends up behind bars all the same.

Upon his release, White returns to the little Minnesota town where he lived before. Clark's description illustrates well the extent to which knowledge leads the Catholic imagination to acknowledge the sinful human condition while at the same time making it capable of celebrating the ultimate triumph of goodness and grace:

> He walked in the places where he had always walked, the places he had walked in when he was a child, and he watched what he remembered of them wear away like flaking paint on the doorsill of the old earth....
>
> He found himself thinking of Ruby Fahey, trying to remember her face and the turn and the hollow in the back of her legs, but try as he might, he could not picture her but could only feel the ache of his emptied memory, the loss of what had recorded the loss of her.
>
> ...Herbert White himself was left alone with only the love of Ruby and without the clear memory of her; and that love was indistinguishable from all the other love and beauty that might be, from what glimmered in the trees, from the light shaking down out of the coloring leaves.[11]

Knowledge admits that bad things happen to good people, sometimes very bad things. It does not encourage us to deny this. But knowledge comprehends a reality much bigger than even the darkest of human injustices. Knowledge views all things in the light of our sharing in the Resurrection, the ultimate triumph of life over death, of good over evil, of justice over injustice. Knowledge hums a little tune to itself, insane though it may seem to be, even in the face of the greatest evils the world has ever known.

Knowledge Is Innocence

Strange and delightful though it may seem, an appropriate symbol for knowledge is the great film comedy team of Stan Laurel and Oliver Hardy. To quote one of their biographers:

> Laurel and Hardy lasted twenty-nine years (1926–55) as an active working team, and yet in all that time their basic gags were not many and they remained the same. Clearly, then, there is a deep, basic quality— dare one call it spiritual?—that kept them in public affection for so long, a quality transcending the mere oddity of physical appearance, pantomimic ability, and gag cleverness. This element permeated their work and it is inherently their brightest glory. The quality is *innocence*.[12]

"The boys," as their fans still refer to them, were masters at playing a couple of characters who fostered no ill will toward the world, regardless of how often it dealt them a losing hand, no matter how often it treated them cruelly. In their films, Stan and Ollie were out simply to do their best, enjoy life, and try to do others a kindness whenever they could. *Way Out West* (1937), the best of their full-length feature films, offers a perfect example of how Laurel and Hardy reflected the spirit of knowledge.

In the film, Stan and Ollie have been sent to an Old West town to deliver news to a young woman named Mary

Roberts—that her father has died but has left her a gold mine. Trusting souls that they are, however, "the boys" end up delivering the title to the mine to the wrong person. Once they discover that they have been hoodwinked, Stan and Ollie are determined to right the wrong and get the title to the mine into the hands of the real Mary Roberts.

Throughout the laugh riot that the rest of the film becomes, Stan and Ollie want nothing more than to do what's right. They wish no harm to anyone, even those who misled them. The point is not that they are naive. On the contrary, they see human nature for what it is, and they recognize lies and selfishness. But Stan and Ollie do not think it is their responsibility to lower the boom on anyone. Vengeance is not their's.

This is how the gift of knowledge works. It gives us insight. It helps us see behind the facade. It shows us the truth. Whereas the world says that "seeing is believing," knowledge says that "believing is seeing."

A Life of Enchantment and Grace

At its most basic, the Holy Spirit's gift of knowledge is, I suggest, the source of what Greeley calls "the Catholic imagination," a way of viewing and experiencing the world. As he writes,

> ...Catholics live in God-haunted houses and an enchanted world. In a world where grace is everywhere, the haunting and enchanting go on constantly. Clearly, the world of the great Catholic artists and writers is enchanted....they see reality the way they do *because* they either grew up Catholic or were attracted to Catholicism as adults by virtue of its enchanting aspects. They reflect an enchantment

that permeates the Catholic community, a haunting that hints powerfully at a salvation guaranteed by pervasive grace [read: the gift of knowledge].13

This gift, this grace we call "knowledge," is the key not just to a way of seeing the world, not just to a vision of life and the cosmos. Even more, it is the key to a Catholic way of living. Do Protestants and those of other religious persuasions not receive the gift of knowledge? They do, I would say, but it seems to "take" in a more powerful way in a Catholic communal context.

To be truly blessed by the Holy Spirit is to know, thanks to the gift of knowledge, that there is far more to reality than merely what we can lay our hands on, than science can quantify, than computers can analyze. There is far more to the truth than surveys can summarize, than polls can proffer. We live—to use Greeley's terms—in an enchanted cosmos, a God-haunted world, and even our homes, or our homelessness if that be the unfortunate case, are filled with the presence of God's love. This is what the gift of knowledge offers and gives, a life of enchantment and grace.

CHAPTER SIX

The Gift of Piety

Think of all the ways that the words *piety* or *pious* tend to be used. If someone described you as "pious," would you be flattered? Maybe not. The word *pious* is often used in a more-or-less derogatory manner. "He/she is way too pious for me." "What a bunch of pious piffle." *Piety* is generally associated with a superficial, quasi-superstitious religion. *Piety* has a bad reputation, as if it were a substitute for authentic faith or real religion. In fact, the word *pious* comes from the Latin *pius,* meaning "dutiful." So an authentically pious person is one who exhibits "religious reverence; [one who is] earnestly compliant in the observance of religion; devout."[1]

That is as far as we can go as long as we limit ourselves to a simple word study. Theologically, of course, there is much more to say and much more to learn about the meaning of the gift of piety. We need to take as our starting point, however, the fact that being "pious" is not generally thought of as behavior to be admired. But it would be a mistake to dismiss genuine piety because the word *pious* has come to describe undesirable religious behavior. In fact, the gift of piety is essential to a mature Christian life.

Piety Helps Us Build Community

The gift of piety has nothing to do with a kind of simple-minded devotionalism carried to extremes, however sincere this behavior may be. Rather, true piety helps us be devoted to God as a true son or daughter. To be "pious" means, first of all, that we actually think of ourselves as sons or daughters of God, and it means we truly do relate to God as our forgiving, loving, and compassionate Father. It takes the gift of piety to pray the Our Father from the heart.

The gift of piety makes it possible for us to include ourselves with Christ, as his adopted brother or sister, in a relationship with the God who reveals himself, through Christ, as our loving Father. The gift of piety comes to us, then, as a result of our baptism into Christ. As brothers and sisters of Christ, we find ourselves in the enviable position of being able to call ourselves children of a God who reveals himself and tender and compassionate. The term Jesus uses in the gospels is the Aramaic "*Abba*," which might be more accurately translated into English as "loving Papa." The gift of piety has nothing to do with a superficial or quasi-superstitious practice of religion and everything to do with what one theologian calls being "filially devoted to God."[2]

Of course, if we are sons and daughters of God and, through baptism, brothers and sisters to Christ, we must also be brothers and sisters to one another. This means that a lively Christian community depends on the gift of piety, on a shared devotion to God and to Christ. It would be difficult, if not impossible, to place too much emphasis on this truth. The much-discussed, much-sought-after value of "community" comes, first of all, from shared devotion. "Community" happens when people share a common dedication to loving and serving God, for this is the source of our shared experience as sons and daughters of God.

Unfortunately, parish and other local Catholic community leaders sometimes get it backward. They think that "community" comes not from a shared filial devotion to God but from various kinds of social and liturgical human interaction. So they organize potluck suppers and Valentine's Day dances. And they encourage a sharing of the sign of peace that becomes a sort of a social chat-fest. Sometimes parishioners are even asked to hold hands while praying the Our Father during Mass, based on a belief that this will encourage a deeper sense of community in parish life as a whole. Or before Mass begins, the presiding priest or music leader will urge everyone to introduce themselves to those around them, interrupting the time that some use to mentally prepare to enter into the communal liturgical experience of the Mass.

Despite all the handholding, shaking of hands, hugging, and so forth, unless what we share with one another is *loving intimacy with the God who is our loving, compassionate, sometimes mother-like Father,* the people around us remain essentially strangers with whom we have shared nothing more than a momentary superficial exchange of greetings. This may seem like a chicken-and-egg issue, but really it's not. Authentic "community" does not come as a result of pretending we are a closely bonded community of faith during Mass. Rather, authentic community happens gradually—when people spend time together in prayerful communion with God.

The most effective way to "build community" is to bring people together for liturgical experiences that eschew superficial expressions of congregational intimacy that does not, in fact, exist—liturgies that provide an authentic shared experience of the risen Christ. From such liturgies a genuine sense of community will develop. Couple with this opportunities for people to share communal devotions, such as a communal praying of the Stations of the Cross during Lent, or communal devotions to Mary or various saints at various appropriate times during the year. Include, too, op- portunities for eucharistic devotions—exposition and adoration of the Blessed Sacrament. Encourage in-home devotional prayer. All this will give rise to an authentic spiritual community in any parish, one in which the liturgical sign of peace is less a frantic search for "intimacy" and more a genuine exchange of the peace of Christ already present in a community of faith.

This is how the gift of piety "works." It leads us prayerfully together to God. This, in turn, gives rise to a true community of faith, which in turn gives meaning to our liturgical and social interactions. If we turn it around and try to make it work the other way—if we try to make community "happen" in ways that bypass the need for authentic prayer—we short-circuit the whole process, and any "community" we may experience feels shallow and phony, or at best incomplete.

The gift of piety relates us to one another by relating us to God as our loving and compassionate Father. If we try to relate to God first by relating to one another, we miss the boat. We simply cannot be in relationship with one another rightly unless we are in relationship with God rightly, and a right relationship with God means allowing the gift of piety to lead us to God as our loving, compassionate Father, as Jesus taught us to do and as the Holy Spirit, through this gift, helps us to do. When we allow this to happen, then genuine Christian community can and will happen.

For lack of better images to rely upon, we can say that we must have a lively "vertical" dimension to our faith in order for the "horizontal" dimension of our faith to be lively, too. A faith community that wants to be all that it can be must make a serious commitment to relate together to God as its top priority. Then the "horizontal" dimension will become all that it can become through the presence of the risen Christ in its midst. No matter how strong the temptation may be to neglect the "vertical" relationship with God, a faith community only shoots itself in the foot, spiritually speaking, if it allows this to happen.

Piety Leads Us to Relationship With All of Creation

We could say that the gift of piety is about faith relationships of all kinds on all levels. It leads us first to God and also, by virtue of our baptism, into loving intimacy with Christ. Through him, of course, we come into loving relationship with Mary, the mother of Jesus, who is now our mother, too. With both intimacy with God our loving Father, and intimacy with Mary, our mother and paradigm of faith, in their proper places, a Christian spirituality for grownups will thrive and lead us to places that we might never have expected to go.

As well, by forming us into a true community of worshipers, piety brings us into ongoing intimacy with the whole communion of saints, in this world and the next. We already implied this when we mentioned intimacy with Mary. This is why Catholics take it for granted that we may petition the saints for prayer on our behalf.

Though the primary orientation of the gift of piety is to help us relate to God as our Father and to one another as brothers and sisters in Christ, piety also opens the human heart to a relationship with the God-created world that respects our earthly environment as a whole. Thus, a pious person would advocate a balanced, properly understood enthusiasm for contemporary efforts to preserve our natural environment and to oppose the destruction of rain forests,

wilderness areas, and other places God's nonhuman crea-
tures need if they are to survive.

The gift of piety helps us to act in ways that respect the
integrity of our natural environment, which is God's gift to
humankind. This includes a thoroughly Franciscan affection
and respect for animals of all kinds and a prayerful attitude
toward forests and other wilderness areas while stopping
short of an inappropriate, unbalanced "nature mysticism"
that mistakes the creature for the Creator. Piety does not
encourage pantheism. Christians worship neither trees nor
animals. While piety may support a "tree hugger" dedication to saving old-growth forests, for example, it will not
do so to the simpleminded extent of forbidding *all* cutting
of old-growth trees. Rather, piety supports the struggle to
cope with environmental issues in ways that respect all the
questions involved, not just one or two of them.

While a Christian may certainly opt to be a vegetarian,
piety will not help him or her do so for simplistic reasons.
Such reasons might include embracing the conviction that
God wants people to eat no meat of any kind, because God
does not want us to kill animals for food. It's fine to be a
vegetarian, but piety leads no one to check his or her brain
at the door or to the condemnation of those who have cho-
sen to eat meat.

The gift of piety also leads us to respect God's creation
in a thoroughly Franciscan way. Saint Francis of Assisi
(c. 1181–1226) turns out to be a kind of patron saint of
piety, our guide in understanding how we should relate to
the natural world, to animals, and to our environment as
a whole. Saint Francis's "Canticle of the Sun" sums up his
theology of creation in general. Here is a particularly good
contemporary translation:

Most High!
Most Mighty!
Most Just Lord!
To you be all praise, glory, worship, and blessing.
Yours they are, and unworthy is our praise.

Be praised, my Lord, in all that you have made!

Be praised for Brother Sun who lights our day.
His beauty, his radiance, his splendor
Surely are but reflections of yours.

Be praised, my Lord, for Sister Moon
and for the stars which shine clearly
decking the heavens with loveliness.

Be praised, my Lord, for our Sister, Water
who humbly serves our many needs
yet is so precious and so pure.

Be praised, my Lord, for our Brother, Fire
who lightens our darkness,
    who brightens and cheers,
who is strength and power.

Be praised, my Lord, for our Mother the Earth
who feeds and tends us,
who sends forth fruit, many-hued flowers,
    and grasses.

Be praised, my Lord,
    in those who forgive for your sake,
and in those who bear troubles and sickness.
O blessed are those who peacefully persevere
To gain a crown from you, Most High Lord.

Be praised, my Lord, for our Sister Death,
Death of the body that none may escape.
Pity those that die in sin.
Blessed are those found walking in virtue.

Praise the Lord! Bless the Lord!
  Give thanks to the Lord!
Serve him with great humility![3]

It is clear from this famous hymn that for Francis, creation takes on its true identity only when we see it in relation to its Creator. Thus, piety helps us see all of creation not in isolation but as a gift coming from our loving Father and as a reflection of God's overwhelming love. The logical response on our part is to do whatever is necessary to care for and respect our world. At the same time, for Saint Francis, creation was not an end in itself. Francis was no nature mystic—he did not worship the natural world.

What Does Piety Have to Say About Creation-Centered Spirituality?

We may ask, does the gift of piety support what is commonly called "creation spirituality"? Typically associated with the works of Matthew Fox, creation spirituality focuses on finding God in and through the natural world, not apart from it. The basic insight upon which creation spir- ituality is based is that "Christian spirituality is not a way out of this world to God, but a way in and with the world to God."[4]

Fox, in particular, opposes what he calls "fall/redemption" spirituality. Indeed, he attributes all kinds of personal and social evils to the dominance of "fall/redemption" spirituality in the Christian tradition. He writes, for example:

The West has been traveling the fall/redemption path for centuries. We all know it; we all have it ingrained in our souls; we have given it ninety-five percent of our energies in churches both Catholic and Protestant. And look where it has gotten us. Into sexism, militarism, racism, genocide against native peoples, biocide, consumerist capitalism, and violent communism. I believe it is time to choose another path. The path that is the most ancient, the most healing, the most feminist of paths, even in the biblical tradition itself.5

From this perspective, evil exists primarily because we have embraced a way of thinking that takes the "fallenness" of human nature for granted, because we have believed that we are radically flawed but redeemed by the life, death, and resurrection of Christ. If, instead, Fox proposes, we were to take the "goodness" of human nature for granted, humankind would, presumably, not be in need of redemption by Christ and, consequently, would never have experienced the evils he enumerates. In other words, we have been afflicted not by original sin but by a *mistaken way of thinking*. Presumably, Christ saves us from this *erroneous way of thinking*.

Creation-centered spirituality has some merit. It reminds us, for example, of the goodness of God's creation in the beginning. It makes the mistake, however, of overlooking the fact that not just people but all of creation is "fallen." Saint Paul expresses it thus:

I consider that the sufferings of this present time are not worth comparing with the glory about to be revealed to us. For the creation waits with eager longing for the revealing of the children of God; for

the creation was subjected to futility, not of its own
will but by the will of the one who subjected it, in
hope that the creation itself will be set free from its
bondage to decay and will obtain the freedom of
the glory of the children of God. We know that the
whole creation has been groaning in labor pains until
now; and not only the creation, but we ourselves,
who have the first fruits of the Spirit, groan inwardly
while we wait for adoption, the redemption of our
bodies (Romans 8:18–23).

It is not just human nature that is "fallen" and in need
of redemption but somehow, mysteriously, all of creation
itself is "in bondage to decay." Proponents of creation-
centered spirituality frequently overlook this scriptural
truth, choosing instead to romanticize nature—including
human nature.

The gift of piety helps us to respect and honor God's
creation without romanticizing it. It helps us to respect the
natural environment and do all we can do to defend it against
abuse, but without acting as if creation is an end in itself.
Creation is indeed the "original blessing," but we must still
take seriously the reality contained in the story of Adam and
Eve. Human nature is "fallen." To be sure, through the life,
death, and resurrection of Christ, redemption is in proc- ess.
But even a quick glance at history tells us that redemption
is far from complete.

Creation takes its proper place in the true scheme of
things only when we refer the creation to its Creator, as Saint
Francis of Assisi did. Yes, creation is a beautiful rainbow
after a summer rain, and there's a magnificent view from
the top of a mountain. But creation is also the tremendous
destructive force of earthquakes, hurricanes, and floods.
Piety helps us enjoy the rainbow, but it also helps us respect

the mystery of nature's destructive power. Piety doesn't romanticize creation, and it doesn't act as if human nature is not radically afflicted by sin. To pretend that both creation and human nature are not "fallen" is naive, at best.

Piety Encourages Devotion

The gift of piety comes into play, also, in our personal spir- ituality. Because piety inclines us to relate to God, it encourages a personal devotional component to our spirituality. Indeed, without this devotional component, faith and spir- ituality risk becoming little more than a "head trip." But here is where we draw closest to the stereotype of the "pious" person, so we need to be cautious and not encourage superficial or escapist "piety."

It is also important to include this devotional element in faith and spirituality as a way to balance the modern emphasis on the communal character of faith and spirituality. Clearly, Christian faith is communal, for it is not possible to be a Christian in isolation from others. According to the *Catechism of the Catholic Church,* "faith needs the community of believers. It is only within the faith of the Church that each of the faithful can believe."[6] The communal component of Christian spirituality preserves a perfectly legitimate form of individualism while preventing, at the same time, a privatized spirituality.

But there are two sides to every coin. Faith also has a private, personal dimension. "The religious sense of the Christian people has always found expression in various forms of piety surrounding the Church's sacramental life...," says the *Catechism.*[7] To neglect this personal, private dimension is to risk simply turning the communal character of faith into a religious echo of the secular herd mentality, which leaves no room for individual creativity or thought.

Without this healthy individualism, the Church might never have contemporary prophets who witness to the word of God when this word conflicts with popular opinion, politics, and culture. But even apart from this relatively rare occurrence, everyone's faith needs a personal, devotional expression that brings her or him into God's presence in solitude. For it is only in solitude that freedom can be preserved. In solitude, alone with God, we come face to face with ourselves and God's love for us. It is in solitude that we discover a depth in ourselves that we may easily overlook if we are never alone. And it is the devotional component of spirituality that helps us find God in solitude.

Thomas Merton, the great mid-twentieth-century Trappist monk, poet, writer, and cultural critic, wrote:

> The need for true solitude is a complex and dangerous thing, but it is a real need. It is all the more real today when the collectivity tends more and more to swallow up the person in its shapeless and faceless mass. The temptation of our day is to equate "love" and "conformity"—passive subservience to the mass-mind or to the organization....
>
> Without a certain element of solitude there can be no compassion because when a man is lost in the wheels of a social machine he is no longer aware of human needs as a matter of personal responsibility. One can escape from men by plunging into the midst of a crowd![8]

The gift of piety leads us into times of authentic solitude, whether this be merely a few minutes in the bathroom, away from a hectic family life, a week on retreat at a monastery, or an afternoon backpacking in the forest or desert. For the faith relationship to be real, it needs a one-on-one dimension. Faith can't be separated from the community of the Church, but it also needs this solitary dimension if it is to be completely real. British philosopher and mathematician Alfred North Whitehead (1861–1947) knew what he was talking about when he said that religion is what you do with your solitude.

Most of the time, piety supports a devotional component of religion and spirituality that is rather ordinary. We simply feel inclined to relate to the Divine Mystery on the level of our emotions as well as on the level of our will and intellect. Piety inclines us to include devotional practices as a part of our everyday lives.

It goes without saying that the Eucharist is the summit and source of Catholic life. Therefore, it is more than appropriate for a Catholic faith and spirituality to include appropriate forms of eucharistic devotional prayer. These may include a simple affection for silent prayer, meditation, and reflection in the presence of the Blessed Sacrament in any church or chapel. But it may also include participation in eucharistic devotional practices such as eucharistic adoration. Care must be taken, however, to ensure that eucharistic devotions do not become overtly connected with ideological or political causes, however praiseworthy they may be.

Piety Gives Us Divine Intimacy

Piety leads us to a lively intimacy with God as loving Father, with the risen Christ, with the Holy Spirit who is the source of this gift, and in a secondary but important sense with the Blessed Virgin. But far from leading us to be "pietistic," the gift of piety instead helps us have a faith that is complete, balanced, and fully human. Piety gives us a love for God and neighbor that is warm, patient, persistent, and courageous.

CHAPTER SEVEN

The Gift of Fear of the Lord

The phrase "fear of the Lord," or its equivalent, occurs more than one hundred times in the Old Testament but only twice in the New Testament (Acts 9:31 and 2 Corinthians 5:11). That should tell us something. Clearly, there is continuity between the Old and New Testaments, and between Judaism and Christianity. This is not to imply, however, that the God of Israel is a stereotypical cold, angry, distant God. Passages such as this one give the lie to any such suggestion: "So now, O Israel, what does the LORD your God require of you? Only to fear the LORD your God, to walk in all his ways, to love him, to serve the LORD your God with all your heart and with all your soul, and to keep the commandments of the LORD your God and his decrees that I am commanding you today, for your own well-being" (Deuteronomy 10:12–13).

The Deuteronomic author(s)/redactor(s) couches "fear of the Lord" in such a way that leaves the reader with no doubt that the God of Israel wants only the people's well-being. Still, the emphasis shifts with the New Testament. Jesus places great emphasis on God as loving and compassionate Father. The *Abba* of Jesus is our *Abba,* too. "God is love," declares the First Letter of John (4:8).

Still, the God of the New Testament is greater than all metaphors. Referring to Christ, the so-called letter to the Hebrews declares that "we have...a high priest, one who is seated at the right hand of the throne of the Majesty in the heavens..." (8:1–2).[1] In other words, it is precisely to help us relate to an absolutely transcendent God that Christ came into human history. Still, God's overwhelming otherness remains. Indeed, from a certain perspective, the Incarnation reaffirms the absolute transcendence of God, for who but an absolutely transcendent God could have the power to come so near?

Fear of the Lord Is Not Terror

The New Testament demonstrates that "fear," in the strict sense of "terror," is an inaccurate way to describe how all disciples of Jesus should relate to God. When both the Old and New Testaments use the phrase *fear of the Lord,* it is not terror that the writers have in mind. "Fear of the Lord" as a gift of the Holy Spirit is related to the virtues of hope, love, and temperance. The purpose of "fear of the Lord" is to help bring *balance* into our lives. Yes, God is our loving and compassionate *Abba.* But a single metaphor can never contain God. God infinitely transcends all human concepts.

Along with love for God should come awe and reverence for God's infinite majesty. God is our *Abba* whom we love, but God is also our God whom we worship and adore. Sometimes, in contemporary spiritual writing, we may get the impression that God is supposed to be our Cosmic Buddy. The Christian perspective is one of balance and tension between God as Divine Mystery and God as loving and compassionate Father. Both are true, and we need to keep both in mind and heart.

"In a healthy spiritual life," writes theologian George P. Evans, "one fears God out of love instead of loving God out of fear."2 This is a good way to understand the balance we need to bring to our understanding of who God is. That is what this discussion is about—our image(s) of God. How we understand and live our faith in every respect depends upon these images. One purpose of the gift of fear of the Lord is to balance those images that bring God close and those that preserve God's transcendence. Fear of the Lord helps us resist the temptation to escape the tension between immanence and transcendence that characterizes a mature faith.

From another perspective, fear of the Lord helps us recognize the limitations of human language when it comes to God. "Since our knowledge of God is limited," says the *Catechism of the Catholic Church*, "our language about him is equally so."3 Therefore, any human concept or image of God is inadequate, even those we find in Scripture. They all fall short of who and what God is for us. Again, from the *Catechism:*

> God transcends all creatures. We must therefore continually purify our language of everything in it that is limited, image-bound or imperfect, if we are not to confuse our image of God "the inexpressible, the incomprehensible, the invisible, the ungraspable" with our human representations [*Liturgy of St. John Chrysostom*, Anaphora]. Our human words always fall short of the mystery of God.4

We "fear" God because we love God, and one way to preserve this understanding is to expose ourselves to images of God in the arts, music, literature, and poetry. We might even say that one task for artists is to help us maintain the connection between God's transcendence and immanence in ways that preserve a God who is both close, distant, and... delightful.

In many of his later poems, twentieth-century American poet Mark Van Doren celebrated a God who is both immanent and transcendent. In "God of Galaxies," for example, he wrote that the old pagan gods, identified with the symbols of the Zodiac, are at a loss now. "The god of galaxies, of burning gases," Van Doren wrote, "May have forgotten Leo and the Bull."

> *But God remembers, and is everywhere.*
> *He even is the void, where nothing shines.*
> *He is the absence of his own reflection*
> *In the deep gulf; he is the dusky cinder*
> *Of pure fire in its prime; he is the place*
> *Prepared for hugest planets: black idea,*
> *Brooding between fierce poles he keeps apart.*

Van Doren continues, describing the indescribability of God, then concludes:

> *...Let us consider it in terror,*
> *And say it without voice. Praise universes*
> *Numberless. Praise all of them. Praise Him.*[5]

The poet's words echo beautifully the spirit of "fear of the Lord." He gazes in awe at the overwhelming majesty of the cosmos, even finding God in "the void" and in "the absence of his own reflection." Then, in the end, he finds himself able in the face of all this to recommend only "terror" and speechlessness. But finally his love for God leaves him no choice but to give voice to his praise: "Praise universes / Numberless. Praise all of them. Praise Him."

This is what the gift of fear of the Lord does: it leads us to sense the overwhelming otherness of God, but it fills us with a love that can only praise God in his transcendence because it brings him so near that—to echo Saint Augustine—God is closer to us than we are to ourselves.

One of the most successful literary efforts to encourage a fear of the Lord that leads to delight occurs at the beginning of Nancy Willard's novel *Things Invisible to See,* a passage I quote frequently. Here are the opening lines:

> In Paradise, on the banks of the River of Time, the Lord of the Universe is playing ball with His archangels. Hundreds of spheres rest like white stones on the bottom of the river, and hundreds rise like bubbles from the water and fly to His hand that alone brings things to pass and gives them their true colors. What a show! He tosses a white ball which breaks into a yellow ball which breaks into a red ball, and in the northeast corner of the Sahara Desert the sand shifts and buries eight camels. The two herdsmen escape, and in a small town in southern Michigan Wanda Harkissian goes into labor with twins. She will name them Ben and Willie, but it's Esau and Jacob all over again.6

The God of Willard's novel is a playful God, whose transcendence expresses itself in delightful ways: he plays ball with his archangels, and the colorful balls they play with come from "the River of Time" and fly out of the river into God's hand "that alone brings things to pass and gives them their true colors." All this adds up to Willard's presentation of God's transcendence as delightful rather than terrifying. Thus, the "fear of the Lord" that she suggests is a kind of awe that is joyful rather than horrified.

Willard's God echoes some words of Saint Paul: "But, as it is written, 'What no eye has seen, nor ear heard, nor the human heart conceived, what God has prepared for those who love him'..." (1 Corinthians 2:9).7 The transcendence of this God inspires joy and delight, anticipation of greater peace and happiness than the human mind can conjure up. Thus, the "fear of the Lord" we find in both Willard's novel and Saint Paul's words is a "fear" that is reluctant to act in ways contrary to the spirit of God's will out of love rather than out of fear and trembling.

Fear of the Lord Reminds Us That God Is Beyond Comprehension

That phrase, however—"fear and trembling"—recalls some other well-known words from Saint Paul's letters: "Therefore, my beloved, just as you have always obeyed me, not only in my presence, but much more now in my absence, work out your own salvation with fear and trembling; for it is God who is at work in you, enabling you both to will and to work for his good pleasure" (Philippians 2:12–13).

Saint Paul provides the balance for the other side of the scales, reminding us that God is beyond *all* images, metaphors, and analogies. We should always have an underlying sense that God is not to be "figured out." We need to regularly remind ourselves, with "fear and trembling," that God cannot be pinned down like an insect on a cosmic specimen board. No matter what we may think we know about God's great love, ultimately we know nothing. As Saint Thomas Aquinas said in the thirteenth century, the first thing we must say about God is that we can say *nothing* about God.8

Fear of the Lord, then, is a gift that helps us be honest about God and with God. It helps us reject any idea of God that is simpleminded or just plain silly, any image of God that neutralizes God as Absolute Mystery, on the one hand, or as Absolute Love, on the other. Fear of the Lord helps us keep imagining a God who is transcendent to the point of immanence and immanent to the point of transcendence.

Some of the poems in Kathleen Norris's book *Little Girls in Church* echo this understanding of fear of the Lord.[9] Appropriately, the poet evokes the spirit of this gift not by writing about God directly, but by evoking God's presence in human experience. The point is that this is *God* in *human* experience. Thus, she reminds us, simultaneously, of how intimate God is with us and how far above us God is. We must pay close attention to see that Norris tells us as much *about* God in these poems as she does about human experience *of* God.

In "The Wedding in the Courthouse," we learn that the narrator of the poem does not like weddings, generally speaking. But one day she is called upon, suddenly, to act as a witness for a thirty-ish couple being married in the county courthouse. At the end of the poem, Norris sets the final scene with Lucille, the justice of the peace; then she concludes with two images, one gritty, the other divine:

> *I can picture Lucille*
> *chain-smoking: surprised*
> *and pleased*
> *to interrupt routine.*
> *And the Deputy Sheriff,*
> *a young man, blushing,*
> *loaded gun in his holster,*
> *arms hanging loose.*
> *He looked at his shoes.*
>
> *It's the words I remember most.*
> *Lucille put out a cigarette*
> *and began: "Dearly beloved,"*
> *and we were!*[10]

The God of this poem is one who evokes true "fear of the Lord." For this God is *God* precisely *in the midst of a young deputy sheriff and a stubbed-out cigarette.* This God manifests himself with two words, "Dearly beloved," and with her final three words—"and we were!"—Norris makes it clear that this is the case. Imagine a God who penetrates such circumstances, a God who can become real and present when a chain-smoking justice of the peace merely clears her throat and speaks the words "Dearly beloved." Such a God is virtually guaranteed to inspire true "fear of the Lord."

As a poet, Norris is a master of metaphors for transcendence-in-immanence. And she teaches us about the deeper meanings of the gift of fear of the Lord. In a poem titled "Emily in Choir," Norris describes a little girl named Emily who holds her father's hand in an abbey church while the monks sing. She asks her father questions, such as "Why do the monks wear peculiar costumes?" She copes with the situation, but to her it seems boring. Then:

> *Brimful of knowledge, Emily shakes my arm:*
> *"They're the monks," she says,*
> *"the men who sing," and she runs*
> *up the aisle, out into the day,*
> *to where the angels are...*
>
> *In the name of the Bee*
> *And of the Butterfly*
> *And of the Breeze Amen!* [11]

Norris gives us another Trinity, the one whistled up in the nineteenth century by another, older Emily than the one in her poem—Emily Dickinson, whom she quotes in italics. This is an image of a God who is intimate with the smallest, most delicate details of his creation, even the bee, the butterfly, and the breeze. This God is the same God we find in an abbey church, yes, among chanting monks. But a little girl rushes out of the church "*to where the angels are,*" and there she finds this God in a way that a little girl is most likely to find him, in the lively details of God's creation.

This God inspires a "fear of the Lord" that is more mind-boggling delight than fear and trembling; or rather, a fear and trembling that is sparked by delight in the face of transcendence-in-immanence—as in the bee, the butterfly, and the breeze.

In yet another of her poems, "The Sky is Full of Blue and of the Mind of God," Norris makes her point in spades, a poetic and theological slam dunk. Waiting at a gas station in the winter's cold, she listens to music from speakers on the outside of the building. In the distance, in the abbey church, she knows that the monks' Mass is not yet over. In the final stanza of the poem, she brings her images together to form a perfect blend of secular and sacred, holy and ordinary:

> *The sky stretches tight, a mandorla of cloud*
> *around the sun. And now*
> *Roy Orbison reaches for the stratosphere:*
> *something about a blue angel.*
> *It is the Sanctus; I know it; I am ready.* 12

Once again, Norris teaches us about the true nature of "fear of the Lord," a gift that has more to do with astonishment than terror, more to do with delight than with whistling in a graveyard. Sometimes the poet's art can be more helpful to us when it comes to understanding this gift than the theologian's craft.

Looking Beyond the Words

The gift of fear of the Lord suffers from its own name, that's what it boils down to. *Fear* is a word we immediately interpret as referring to a state of emotional distress in the face of some danger to our personal safety. Sometimes, the Scriptures use the word in this sense, of course. In Joshua 9:24, for example, the Gibeonites excuse their behavior to Joshua by saying,

> Because it was told to your servants for a certainty that the LORD your God had commanded his servant Moses to give you all the land, and to destroy all the inhabitants of the land before you; so we were in great fear for our lives because of you, and did this thing.

In another instance, in Luke 21:26, Jesus declares about the coming of the Son of Man:

> People will faint from fear and foreboding of what is coming upon the world, for the powers of the heavens will be shaken.

The other scriptural meaning of *fear,* however, is the one we need to keep in mind when we speak of the Holy Spirit's gift of fear of the Lord. This meaning "relates to allegiance to and regard for deity."[13] The human act of *worship* is rooted in this gift, and true worship includes profound respect and awe.[14] Fear of the Lord means having the capacity to worship God with deep respect. This "fear" implies obedience, love, trust, and sometimes the sense of deep joy and profound delight we discussed above.

People of faith sometimes take all this for granted. Yet we live in an era when countless people are deeply distrustful of the very idea of worship, of bowing down, figuratively speaking, to God. Many people are either indifferent to God or live a kind of practical atheism that implies that if there is a God, he has no concern for everyday human happenings and certainly has no particular interest in me and my joys and sorrows.

Fear of the Lord is a tremendous gift because it makes true worship possible, that is, it makes it possible for faith to be more than a theory—to be, in fact, loving intimacy with God. If we receive this gift, it becomes possible to love God, trust God, and want to obey God. It becomes possible to delight in God's love and abandon ourselves to the loving action of God in our lives without acting as if we have God, the Divine Mystery, all figured out.

Today, there is an increasingly common understanding that the metaphors, images, and analogies we use for God have intrinsic importance. It's true that metaphors are all we have when it comes to talking about God. But still, a metaphor is only a metaphor; it is not the reality the metaphor refers to. Fear of the Lord should help us keep our metaphors for God in perspective, to remember their limitations. Can we do better than to cherish the metaphors biblical tradition has given us as the best that can be said about God?

This is one of the most important functions of fear of the Lord. It lets God be God. It helps us resist the temptation to fashion a God in our own images. It overcomes the arrogance of thinking that we are within our rights when we crash into the language of the Scriptures and the liturgy like a bull in a china shop, determined to "improve" on what we find there.

Fear of the Lord brings the gift of "littleness," if you will. It helps us to sidestep the temptation to be so arrogant as to think, for example, that we can improve on the images and metaphors for God that are found in the Scriptures. The idea of "submission" is not a popular one. The notion that at some point faith requires us to bow to an authority greater than our own is likely to evoke cries of "Foul!" from more than a few people of faith today. But fear of the Lord includes the capacity for this kind of spiritual submission. We're not talking about submission to human authority. We're not even talking about submission to legitimate Church teaching authority, where issues of conscience come into play and are anything but irrelevant. Rather, the authority we speak of here is the authority of Scripture and sacred Tradition, which for Roman Catholics cannot be separated.[15] Of course, the idea is not to encourage a fundamentalist reading of Scripture. But fear of the Lord helps us accept Scripture's images, analogies, and metaphors for God as expressing as fully as possible who God is for us.

In other words, God, the Divine Mystery, is beyond all metaphors, images, and analogies, so fear of the Lord helps us "make do" with those references we've been given and let it go at that. In this sense, fear of the Lord enables us to submit to the authority of the Scriptures. Rather than being a limiting thing, or a shackling of our spiritual capacities, this submission actually liberates us. It frees us from an oppressive "need" to constantly wrestle with the images, analogies, and metaphors for God in the Scriptures in an attempt to force them into conformity with a merely contemporary theological ideology. Instead, if we can accept these images of God, we can move on with our efforts to apply the spirit of the Scriptures to the here and now concrete details of everyday life.

What Is Fear of the Lord?

So here is what we are saying: The Holy Spirit's gift of fear of the Lord isn't about fear, in the usual sense of the word, at all. Fear of the Lord might better be renamed "astonishment at the Lord." The gift of astonishment at the Lord is the gift that helps us realize that God is not our divine lap dog. Rather, God simply *is,* and God *is* here, there, and everywhere. In our deepest center, and in the farthest reaches of outer space playing and dancing with the stars and planets in his heart. God is so great and so good that he should spark amazement, awe, and down-on-your-knees-ness regularly. That's what the gift of fear of/astonishment at the Lord is about.

At the same time, this gift helps us let God be God; it helps us resist the temptation to put God in any kind of box, whether the box be ideological, theological, political, driven by piety, or merely fashioned from well-meant intentions. Astonishment at the Lord frees us to rely on the God whose reflection we find in the ancient Scriptures. At the same time, this gift gives us permission to play with images of God all we like in everyday life.

Here, says the gift of astonishment at the Lord, is what God is like: a playful child, an indulgent father, a compassionate mother, a shepherd looking for a lost sheep, a woman searching for a lost coin, a father waiting for his wandering son's return, an old woman, a bright star in the night sky, a little blue wildflower, a teenager with shocking sartorial habits, a mirror, a sad song or a joyful song, a concerto by Bach, Mozart's *Requiem*, punk rock music, Mount Everest, a sleeping infant, a playful puppy, a long, long walk...there is no end to what God is like, declares the gift of fear of the Lord. "Don't fence me in," sings the God of this gift. "Just let me wander over yonder out beneath the western skies...." Oh yes, don't forget that our God is also a smiling God, a God with a sense of humor. How could anyone see a duck-billed platypus and not know that God thinks that one is a real knee-slapper? How could anyone gaze at a giraffe and not understand that God thinks that one is a major rib-tickler? How could anyone slice open an avocado, see that the seed is *way* too big, and not know that this, too, is one of God's jokes?

The gift of fear of the Lord, or astonishment at the Lord, is the gift that helps us let God be God and not take our ideas of God too seriously. That's the long and the short of it.

CHAPTER EIGHT

The "Fruits" of the Holy Spirit

One of the lists—and there were more than a few of them—that Roman Catholic children were once required to memorize was the list of the "fruits" of the Holy Spirit. As traditionally formulated, the list included twelve "fruits":

1. *Charity*
2. *Joy*
3. *Peace*
4. *Patience*
5. *Kindness*
6. *Goodness*
7. *Long-suffering*
8. *Humility*
9. *Fidelity*
10. *Modesty*
11. *Continence*
12. *Chastity*[1]

This list was based on Galatians 5:22–23 in the Douay-Rheims translation of the Bible, the version approved for use by Roman Catholics prior to the 1943 encyclical of Pope

Pius XII, *Divino Afflante Spiritu*, which encouraged modern translations of the Bible from the original languages. The Douay-Rheims translation was based on the Latin Vulgate, the Latin translation of the Bible begun by Saint Jerome (347–420) and later completed by others. Final revisions of the Vulgate were completed in the late sixteenth century.[2]

Here is how the actual Douay-Rheims text reads: "But the fruit of the Spirit is, charity, joy, peace, patience, benignity, goodness, longanimity, mildness, faith, modesty, continency, chastity. Against such there is no law."[3]

As you can see, the traditional list of "fruits" uses different terminology. More significantly, the list of "fruits" in the Douay-Rheims version included the last three items on the traditional list (Modesty, Continence, Chastity), whereas you will not find these three in any contemporary version of the New Testament. See the *New Revised Standard Version*, for example: "By contrast, the fruit of the Spirit is love, joy, peace, patience, kindness, generosity, faithfulness, gentleness, and self-control. There is no law against such things."

Granted, then, that the version in Galatians includes fewer items, and a contemporary translation is somewhat different from the traditional list. All the same, for discussion purposes we will follow the traditional list while updating a few of the names for the "fruits."

The first thing we need to clarify is the meaning of *fruits*. This rather maudlin term simply refers to the *effects* of the Holy Spirit's activity in human beings. All of these are signs, or "symptoms," if you will, of an ongoing conversion to Christ. Thus, the effects of the gifts of the Holy Spirit, with which most of this book concerns itself, are love, joy, peace, patience, kindness, generosity, faithfulness, gentleness, self-control, modesty, continence, and chastity. Now we may continue with a more detailed reflection on each of the "fruits," or effects, of the gifts of the Holy Spirit.

Love

The love that is an effect of the Holy Spirit's activity is not, first of all, romantic love, although it may include romantic love, too. The first meaning of *love* here is the love that results from an experience of God's love and mercy. It's easy to talk about this experience, but it is an experience even sincere churchgoers sometimes find difficult to understand. Mention experiences of God's love and mercy, and chances are a significant number of people in your audience won't have a clue as to what you are referring to. This is because the dominant culture is so secularized that it leaves people ill-equipped to recognize God's presence in their lives.

For many people, God is a concept but not a reality. In our everyday lives, many of us never think about God or consider that he may be active in our experiences and in the workaday world. When it comes to "the real world" of family, work, and paying the bills, even many churchgoers live what might be called a kind of "practical atheism." For example, many young adults make relationship decisions with little or no sense of God's loving presence in their lives, with little or no sense of a traditional respect for one another's God-given dignity that would, for example, preclude sexual activity outside of marriage. Cohabitation—before being "nonjudgmental" came into vogue, it was often called "shacking up"—is a taken-for-granted option, and many, perhaps most, young adults today see nothing objectionable, much less sinful, about it.

This and much more about modern life can be traced to a widespread lack of sensitivity to God's presence in the world and in human experience. No matter if parents model traditional Christian beliefs about sex and marriage, it's difficult for young adults to think of sex as sacred and reserved to marriage if they have few or no experiences they can identify as sacred. It's next to impossible to think of sex as sacred if, all your life, the dominant popular culture has told you in hundreds of ways that sex is for fun and that unmarried people have as much of a right to sex as married people.

This leaves us with a big problem, then, if we want to talk about the love that is one of the effects of the Holy Spirit's activity in human life. If people have no experiences that they can identify with "God," how can they have an experience of God's love and mercy that makes it possible for them, in turn, to love with the love that is one of the "fruits" of the Holy Spirit? Where does this leave us? Perhaps feeling more helpless than anything else. There are no easy answers to issues such as this one, but asking the question is valuable in itself, even if we don't have a truckload of answers all ready to go.

Perhaps the best response to widespread "practical atheism" is for those for whom God is real, and for whom experiences of God's love are real, to renew their dedication to prayer and renew their dedication to a life of humble, honest, courageous faith. Indeed, the more people who do this, the more likely it is that their prayers will change the world.

Perhaps the main issue for people today is not so much whether God is real or not, but whether God is *personal* or not. Many people think of God as more of a distant "force" of some kind. The effect of the Holy Spirit's activity in human life that we call love depends on an experience of God not as an impersonal, distant, uninvolved "force," but as a close, intimate, warm, personal reality. The only way people will believe that this is so is for those who experience God as personal and close to live their lives in correspondingly appropriate ways. In other words, the only way people will believe in a loving God is for people of faith to be loving people.

For people of faith, the gifts of the Holy Spirit must lead to lives of practical love. Otherwise, it will be nearly impossible for other people to take seriously the claim that there is a personal God who invites us to surrender ourselves to loving intimacy with himself and to community with one another.

Joy

The second effect of the Holy Spirit's activity in our lives is an ongoing experience of joy that is not subject to shifting moods or the conditions of our lives. The joy that characterizes a Christian life is not a giddy ephemeral effervescence of an emotional kind. Rather, it is a deeper spiritual experience that remains, regardless of anything else that may be happening. This joy is the kind we see most clearly in the lives of saints, both well known and obscure.

One of the best modern examples of this joy may be found in the life of Saint Maximilian Kolbe, the Franciscan priest who volunteered to give his life so that another man might live in the World War II Nazi death camp, Auschwitz. Witnesses later testified that right up to his last moments, as he lay dying of starvation, Father Kolbe was a man of joy. One witness said:

> Like many others, I crawled at night in the infirmary on the bare floor to the bed of Father Maximilian. The greeting was moving. We exchanged some impressions on the frightful crematorium. He encouraged me, and I confessed. Discouragement and doubt threatened to overwhelm me; but I still wanted to love. He helped me to strengthen my belief in the final victory of good. "Hatred is not creative," he whispered to me. "Our sorrow is necessary that those who

live after us may be happy." His reflections on the mercy of God went straight to my heart. His words to forgive the persecutors, and to overcome evil with good, kept me from collapsing into despair.[4]

Saint Maximilian was a man of joy in the midst of terrible, inhuman suffering and misery. His example is extreme, of course, but it illustrates the point: that the joy that is an effect of the Holy Spirit's activity in human life does not depend on a life free of trouble or pain.

Peace

Saint Maximilian would be just as good an example of the peace that is another "fruit" of the Holy Spirit. For peace fears no force of evil nor evident dangers. Ultimately, peace has no fear even of death. Jesus himself speaks of this peace in the Gospel of John: "Peace I leave with you; my peace I give to you. I do not give to you as the world gives. Do not let your hearts be troubled, and do not let them be afraid" (14:27).

The peace that is one of the "fruits" of the Holy Spirit is not the peace that "the world" gives. In the Gospel of John, "the world" means the dominant culture, together with the economic and political systems to which it is linked, to the extent that it is opposed to the spirit and goals of the gospel. So the peace that "the world" gives is a peace that depends on personal safety, on financial forms of security, and on the approval of others. "The world" is concerned, ultimately, with personal security and social approval rather than union with Christ and the will of God.

The peace that is a "fruit" of the Holy Spirit, on the contrary, is a peace that *depends* upon union with Christ and the will of God. People of faith may often have the peace that the world gives along with the peace that comes from the Holy Spirit. But there may well be times when faith requires the sacrifice of the world's peace in order to preserve the Spirit's peace.

Because the Spirit's peace is the greater, people of faith are willing, if necessary, to put themselves at personal risk to promote the cause of Christ. In the case of Saint Maximilian Kolbe and many other saints, famous and unknown, it became necessary. Whenever faith requires active opposition to the forces of evil in the world, then personal risk becomes necessary. This may include opposition to political, economic, social, and cultural forces, all for the sake of the gospel and for the peace that surpasses all understanding.

The Spirit's peace is one that transcends or is much deeper than immediate circumstances. It is a peace that can co-exist with personal suffering, affliction, even outright persecution. It is a peace that recognizes the shallow forms of peace that "the world" can give. It is a peace that also weeps in the face of the many addictions that claim people with their siren call, bringing the deepest kind of inner freedom, never the kinds of slavery that addictions deliver.

Patience

Patience is one of the most difficult effects of the Holy Spirit's presence and activity to find in our culture. Indeed, the emotional capacity for patience is not one of the primary characteristics of people who live in the so-called developed nations. Rather, we experience stresses that result from anxious concerns to be where we are not, to have what we do not, to be who we are not, and to get there faster today than we did yesterday. Patience requires the ability to *wait* and to do so with equanimity, peacefully and without anxiety. The patience that is a "fruit" of the Holy Spirit has much in common with the Buddhist ideal of "mindfulness," a simple being present to the present moment and all that it brings.[5]

The Spirit's patience is the capacity to be satisfied with what we already have, to be able to live in the present moment without longing for the future. The present moment is both good and valuable in itself and, pregnant with the future, is worth treasuring for itself. Patience embraces *now* for its own sake; it does not reject *now* because it is not yet *then*—an hour from now, a day from now, a week or month or year or five years from now.

Patience characterizes a life that is *grown up,* a life that is mature in the fullest sense of the word. For only an adult can be patient, can *be* in the now. The patient person has the capacity to let the yeast work in the bread and allow it to rise, can wait nine months for the baby without cultivating an impossible longing for the waiting to be over, can wait for the traffic light to change from red to green without grinding his or her teeth. The patient person knows that the waiting, the being in the now, is good and is a gift in itself.

Kindness

Kindness is one "fruit" of the Holy Spirit's action that can seem "soft," a way of acting most suitable to those who find themselves in the presence of those who are weak and defenseless—little children, people who are seriously ill, and so forth. Nevertheless, there seems to be a widespread lack of simple kindness today. Everyone appreciates being treated kindly, but how often do we consciously focus on being kind to others and to ourselves?

Kindness is one of those words we do well to trace back to its dictionary definition, so common is the word and so frequently misunderstood:

kind (kīnd) adj. **kind-er, kind-est. 1.** Of a friendly,
generous, or warm-hearted nature. **2.** Showing sympathy or understanding; charitable: *a kind word.* **3.**
Humane; considerate: *kind to animals.* **4.** Forbear
ing; tolerant: *Our neighbor was very kind about the
window we broke.* **5.** Generous; liberal: *kind words
of praise.* **6.** Agreeable; beneficial: *a dry climate kind
to asthmatics.* [Middle English, natural, kind, from
Old English *gecynde*, natural. See *gen-*.]6

So the first meaning of *kind* is simply to be "friendly, generous, or warm-hearted." Think about it for a moment.
Imagine if everyone you met today was "friendly, generous,
or warm-hearted." Talk about a major social revolution!
Imagine for just a moment if everyone you met today was
sympathetic and understanding, humane and considerate,
forbearing and tolerant, generous...and *liberal!*

The more open to and filled with the gifts of the Holy
Spirit we are, the more *liberal* we will be. Does this amount
to a scriptural endorsement for a political position. Probably not. Still, we would need to say that there is a sense in
which even political conservatives are called to be liberal,
meaning "free," when it comes to being charitable, understanding, generous, warm-hearted, and so forth. No one can
justify stinginess when it comes to being kind. Frequently,
the problem we have is that we are selective about whom
we are kind to. We don't mind being kind to our friends
and those we love.

On second thought, sometimes the very ones we "forget"
to be kind to are those we love! We tend to take the other
members of our family for granted. Imagine making it a
point to be kind to your spouse today. Imagine making a
special effort to be kind to your children. Imagine focusing
on being kind to your co-workers.

The point, of course, is that kindness is anything but a "soft" concern. Being kind requires a will of steel sometimes. Kindness is definitely a "fruit" of the Holy Spirit's activity with which we need the Holy Spirit's help.

Goodness

If ever a human characteristic or quality had a bad reputation, this is it. Who wants to be *good* nowadays? Calling someone "a good person" is to tar and feather him or her with faint praise. "Cool," yes. "Savvy," yes. But "good"? Give us all a break, puh-leeze. Goodness just isn't *cool*.

All the same, goodness is one of the "fruits" of the Holy Spirit. This leaves us with two tasks. First, we need to understand what "goodness" really is. Second, we need to acknowledge that, ironic though it is, there is bound to be something countercultural about goodness.

Goodness is perhaps best understood through various synonyms, such as uprightness, decency, morality, rectitude, righteousness, rightness, virtue, virtuousness. A good person is all of these. Which brings us back to our original problem. The trouble with "goodness" is that it seems to refer to a person who is basically a self-righteous goody two shoes. But perhaps we still don't understand goodness.

The trouble with everything we know about goodness so far is that it seems to label a person who is no fun to be around. It seems that a "good" person could be little more than a prude, someone with no sense of humor, someone who could never "let his or her hair down" and "have a good time," someone who would never "let it all hang out" and dance the night away. A "good" person would never "rock 'n' roll" in any sense of the word—which just goes to show how out of focus the common understanding of goodness really is.

Goodness is not a characteristic of a person who is emotionally, socially, or culturally shriveled, and adult goodness is not the same as the goodness appropriate to a child or an adolescent. We might, instead, define a good person as one who is "hale and hearty" in every respect. If you are a good person, it simply means that you are not the center of your own universe. Rather, you are eager for life and ready to celebrate it at the drop of a hat. You believe in self-sacrifice, but you don't believe in being anybody's doormat. A good person knows how to whistle a cheerful tune while walking down the sidewalk on a beautiful spring morning or in the middle of a snowstorm. Goodness characterizes people who deal as well with suffering and setbacks as they do with health and success, which leads naturally to...

Long-Suffering

Here is a "fruit" of the Holy Spirit that, in our time as in all times, is about as popular as acne. *Long-suffering* means "patient endurance of wrongs or difficulties." You want to know the exact opposite of the long-suffering person? The exact opposite is the whiner. Now, don't get me wrong. Personally, I think that sometimes whining can be a great release, a way to relieve some stress, as long as it's done in a humorous way. As soon as whining becomes serious—whining about difficulties you have to deal with—then it becomes sincerely meant whining, not just kidding around, and then it's the exact opposite of being long-suffering. Then you are being a major-league whiner.

There is also the person who "patiently" endures hard times...but makes sure everyone knows about it. This person is not exhibiting long-suffering because now he or she is demonstrating something suspiciously similar to self-righteousness and setting himself or herself up as a self-declared "martyr." If everyone knows how patiently we are enduring, then we're no longer long-suffering, we're now just a pain in the derrière.

Long-suffering is a difficult gift because as soon as we no longer keep our troubles to ourselves, as soon as we feel a need to broadcast how long-suffering we are, we are no longer long-suffering. To be long-suffering does not mean we never talk with anyone else about our troubles. It simply means that we don't make a big production out of it. For example, a truly long-suffering person is someone with a chronic illness who does not make a big secret of it, but neither does it become that person's sole topic of conversation. Life goes on....

Long-suffering is aptly named because it truly does mean to suffer for a long time, however great or minor the suffering may be. There is an intimate mystical connection between the "fruit" of long-suffering and the Christian experience of the cross of Christ. We all have "crosses" in life, but the long-suffering person gets to know the cross of Christ in a more intimate way. Of course in the life of Christian faith, there is no cross without resurrection; the two go hand in hand. Therefore, the long-suffering person, in ways others may find difficult to grasp, experiences and knows the new resurrection life in real but mysterious ways. Truly long-suffering people of faith may find it impossible to explain to others, but their experience of the resurrection of Christ in the midst of their experience of the cross of Christ is utterly real.

Finally, it is important to note that "long-suffering" is not an effect of the Holy Spirit's activity in, for example, a marriage where one spouse regularly abuses the other spouse physically or emotionally. The same goes for a marriage in which one spouse abuses alcohol or other drugs. Long-suffering is an effect of the Holy Spirit's activity only when it involves living with trouble, hard times, or suffering that is beyond the control of anyone concerned.

Humility

Humility is one "fruit" of the Holy Spirit that people frequently misunderstand. The Latin root of the word *humility* is *humus*, "ground." To borrow a colloquialism, a humble person is simply one who "has his or her feet on the ground." A humble person is "down to earth." As an effect of the Holy Spirit's activity, humility has nothing to do with low self-esteem or "putting ourselves down." When the Holy Spirit is involved, humility means we don't think of ourselves as any more, or less, than we are. If one is a world-famous, highly gifted brain surgeon, and someone compliments that person on the good he or she has accomplished, she or he wouldn't reject the compliment. Neither, however, do we allow words of praise to give us an inflated sense of ourselves. The world-famous brain surgeon has just as many faults as the next person.

Being humble means we can identify with the attitude of the cartoon character Popeye the sailor man: "I yam what I yam, and that's all what I yam...."

Humility is the close companion of truth, in this case the truth about ourselves. Whatever is true about us, both the good and the bad, is what we admit to as a humble person. Of course, the most important truth is that God loves us unconditionally. Therefore, we have no cause, ever, to let others' opinions hold much sway over our feelings about ourselves. When people despise us, it shouldn't make much difference. When people praise and admire us, that shouldn't make much difference, either. Both should be like water off the proverbial duck's back.

Humility never calls attention to itself. "True humility makes no pretense of being humble," said Saint Francis de Sales in the early seventeenth century, "and scarcely ever utters words of humility." True humility never remarks on how unworthy it is or how insignificant its accomplishments are. The truly humble person acknowledges the kindness of the person who offers admiration and praise...then forgets about it.

Fidelity

Fidelity, a great effect of the Holy Spirit's activity in people, means much more than being faithful. It also means being reliable. It means others can count on us to deliver. It means that when we say we are going to do something, we by golly do it. It applies to big promises, vows, and commitments, of course, including the "biggies" such as marriage. Fidelity in marriage means remaining faithful no matter what. It means we believe in that bugaboo of the modern spirit, permanent commitments.

At the same time, fidelity is quite the everyday "fruit" of the Holy Spirit's presence. The faithful person is the one who simply "hangs in there" from one day to the next, staying in the saddle for the long haul, but one day at a time. When fidelity is alive and kicking, it means that not only do we stay faithful to our big promises but that we can be counted on to follow through on our everyday promises. If we say we will be someplace at a certain time or do something for someone, then only totally unavoidable circumstances will keep us from honoring our commitments. In this respect, fidelity means that we have a sense of respect for others, as well.

Modesty

Now here's a "fruit" of the Holy Spirit that can pull us in several directions at once. Basically, modesty refers to a certain reserve, a certain inclination to not "let it all hang out," whether in one's attire or in one's behavior.

Culturally acceptable standards of modesty with regard to attire change. In the late nineteenth century, for example, both men and women at the beach wore "bathing garb" that covered the person from neck to ankles. Gradually, these standards of modesty gave way to practicality, to the point that beachwear has become what by nineteenth-century standards would be scandalous, to say the least. Most people, of course, do not wear the scantiest of swimwear. For one thing, most people have fairly ordinary bodies that would not look great in a greatly abbreviated bathing suit.

Swim wear aside, however, one may venture to say that what constitutes modesty in dress remains debatable. During the 1950s, Catholic girls and women were sometimes urged to dress in a "Mary-like" manner, but we don't hear much about this as we lurch into the twenty-first century. Perhaps it's enough to say that most people have enough common sense to dress in ways that respect both themselves and the Creator of the human physiognomy.

When it comes to modesty, the more important issue is behavior. As a "fruit" of the Holy Spirit, modesty is close to humility. It simply means being ourselves, not acting as if we are superior beings. At the same time, the modest person does not try to hide his or her talents, gifts, and abilities. The modest person cultivates and uses the gifts that God has given him or her.

Continence

The "fruit" of continence is simply the inclination to practice moderation and self-restraint in all kinds of ways. Continence means we integrate the various human appetites in a balanced manner into our lives. We eat in moderation. We control ourselves when it comes to sexual activity. We are in charge of our appetites; our appetites are not in charge of us.

Of course, sometimes continence means eating for the sake of good health when we may feel inclined not to eat. We may find that continence means *not* playing golf when our spouse needs our presence, for the sake of a healthy marriage. Continence is not always about *not* doing something. Sometimes it's about *doing* something.

Continence isn't just about drinking and eating, either. Continence is about moderation and self-control in all areas of human life and activity, from physical exercise to sleep, from reading to watching television, and from hobbies to work. Continence is about balance.

Chastity

Where, oh where, has chastity gone? One almost despairs of chastity's getting any respect in the dominant culture of our time. The "fruit" of the Holy Spirit called chastity is the virtue of using God's wonderful gift of sexuality in ways appropriate to one's calling. Sexuality has an appropriate place in the life of a single person, a married person, and a celibate person, and we're not just talking about the physical expression of love. Physical expressions of love are chaste and virtuous in marriage, but there are some physical expressions of love that are virtuous for an engaged couple, too.

"Sexuality" refers primarily to the human capacity to relate in warm, loving ways to other people. A celibate priest or religious will be chaste by expressing warm human love for others in nongenital ways. But the priest or religious will be, all the same, a warm, loving person. Celibacy is no excuse to distance oneself emotionally from other people of either sex.

Chastity means being a sexual person in appropriate ways. We are chaste in certain ways with a spouse, if we are married. In other ways with friends, and in yet other ways with casual acquaintances. We are chaste in a different way with men than we are with women.

Chastity does not mean being a cold, unfeeling, sexually shriveled person. Rather, being chaste means relating as a sexual person to all the people in our lives in warm, caring ways that are appropriate to our relationships with each person, whoever he or she may be.

Notes

Introduction

1. Barbara A. Finan, "Holy Spirit," in Richard P. McBrien, general ed., The HarperCollins Encyclopedia of Catholicism (San Francisco: HarperSanFrancisco, 1995), 630.

2. *Catechism of the Catholic Church*, n. 40, n. 42.

3. Feminist theologians often insist that the "Father" and "Son" metaphors no longer adequately express the fullness of a Christian faith experience and must be balanced by an equal use of feminine metaphors for God. After some two thousand years of using the traditional masculine metaphors, together with their scriptural foundations, however, the viability of feminine metaphors for God in Christian faith and worship remains to be seen. See John W. Miller, *Calling God"Father"*: *Essays on the Bible, Fatherhood & Culture* (Mahwah, N.J.: Paulist Press, 1999).

4. *Catechism of the Catholic Church*, n. 43.

5. See George P. Evans, "Gifts of the Holy Spirit," in Michael Downey, ed., *The New Dictionary of Catholic Spirituality* (Collegeville, Minn.: The Liturgical Press, 1993), 436.

6. See Gerald O'Collins, S.J., *The Tripersonal God: Understanding and Interpreting the Trinity* (Mahwah, N.J.: Paulist Press, 1999), 166.

Chapter 1

1. See John W. Miller, *Calling God "Father"*: *Essays on the Bible, Fatherhood & Culture* (Mahwah, N.J.: Paulist Press, 1999), 5: "*Not once in biblical tradition is God ever spoken of as 'she' or 'her' or regarded as genderless. On the other hand, God is not portrayed there simply as male, either, but as a father whose tenderness and compassion are often mother-like. In no instance does this imply that God has become a mother-figure to his worshipers. The uniformity of the canonical representation of God as father is one of its most notable feaures.*" (Italics in original.)

2. Thomas Aquinas, *Summa Theologiae: A Concise Translation,* ed. by Thomas McDermott (Westminster, Md.: Christian Classics, 1989) I:1, 6.

3. Ibid., II:8, 4.

4. Thomas Merton, "Wisdom," in *The Collected Poems of Thomas Merton* (New York: New Directions, 1977), 279.

Chapter 2

1. Excerpted from *American Heritage Talking Dictionary.* Copyright 1997 by The Learning Company, Inc. All rights reserved.

2. George P. Evans, "Gifts of the Holy Spirit," in Michael Downey, ed., *The New Dictionary of Catholic Spirituality* (Collegeville, Minn.: The Liturgical Press, 1993), 437.

3. *Catechism of the Catholic Church,* n. 2290.

4. Robert A. Krieg, "Incarnation," in Richard P. McBrien, general ed., *The HarperCollins Encyclopedia of Catholicism* (San Francisco: Harper San Francisco, 1995), 659.

5. See John Deedy, *A Book of Catholic Anecdotes* (Allen, Texas: Thomas More Publications, 1997), 132.

6. Ronda De Sola Chervin, *Quotable Saints* (Ann Arbor, Mich.: Servant Publications, 1992), 122.

Chapter 3

1. See George P. Evans, "Gifts of the Holy Spirit," in Michael Downey, ed., *The New Dictionary of Catholic Spirituality* (Collegeville, Minn.: The Liturgical Press, 1993), 437–38.

2. Thomas Aquinas, *Summa Theologiae: A Concise Translation,* ed. by Thomas McDermott (Westminster, Md.: Christian Classics, 1989), 338.

3. Anne Lamott, *Traveling Mercies: Some Thoughts on Faith* (New York: Anchor Books, 1999), 179–80.

4. Ibid., 180.

5. Ludwig Bemelmans. *Madeline.* Story and pictures by Ludwig Bemelmans. New York: Simon & Schuster, 1939.

6. James M. Barrie. *Peter Pan.* New York, 1928.

7. A. A. Milne. *Winnie-the-Pooh.* New York: E. P. Dutton & Company, 1926.

8. See Henry David Thoreau, *Walden.* First published in the United States by Ticknor and Fields, 1854. Available in many editions from various publishers.

9. Caroline Rush. *Further Tales of Mr. Pengachoosa*. New York: Crown, 1967.

10. L. Frank Baum. *The Wizard of Oz*. New York: G. M. Hill Co, 1900.

11. Hugh Lofting. *The Voyages of Doctor Doolittle*. New York: Fred A. Stokes Co., 1922.

12. See *The Story of a Soul: The Autobiography of St. Thérèse of Lisieux*, trans. by John Clarke, O.C.D. (Washington, D.C.: ICS Publications, 1976), 134.

13. From a personal conversation with the author.

14. Antoine de Saint-Exupéry. *The Little Prince*, translated from the French by Katherine Woods. New York: Reynel & Hitchcock, 1943.

15. Richard Wilbur. *Opposites*. New York: Harcourt Brace Jovanovich, 1973.

16. Beatrice Schenk de Regniers. *The Enchanted Forest*. New York: Atheneum, 1974.

Chapter 4

1. George P. Evans, "Cardinal Virtues," in Michael Downey, ed., *The New Dictionary of Catholic Spirituality* (Collegeville, Minn.: The Liturgical Press, 1993), 116.

2. Jon Winokur, ed., *The Portable Curmudgeon Redux* (New York: Dutton Books, 1992), 54.

3. See Dick Westley, "Sexuality," in Michael Downey, ed. *The New Dictionary of Catholic Spirituality* (Collegeville, Minn.: The Liturgical Press, 1993), 877–83.

4. Ibid., 882.

5. Ibid., 882.

6. Author's personal recollection of a news report.

7. See Hans Küng, *Mozart: Traces of Transcendence* (Grand Rapids, Mich.: Wm. B. Eerdmans Publishing Co., 1991).

8. Quoted in Cliff Edwards, *Van Gogh and God: A Creative Spiritual Quest* (Chicago: Loyola Press, 1989), 162.

9. Quoted in ibid., 160.

10. Walter J. Burghardt, S.J., *Long Have I Loved You: A Theologian Reflects on His Church* (Maryknoll, N.Y.: Orbis Books, 2000), 418–19.

11. Flannery O'Connor, *Collected Works,* Sally Fitzgerald, ed. (New York: The Library of America, 1988), 1163.

12. Flannery O'Connor, *The Presence of Grace and Other Book Reviews,* Leo J. Zuber, comp., Carter W. Martin, ed. and introduction (Athens, Ga.: The University of Georgia Press, 1983), 148.

13. Graham Greene, *The Heart of the Matter,* in Philip Stratford, ed., *The Portable Graham Greene,* rev. ed. (Nework: Penguin Books, 1994), 304–5.

14. John Stewart, "The Long Train of Dreams," copyright 1999 by John Stewart. Homecoming Records, P.O. Box 2050 Malibu, CA 90265.

15. Ibid.

Chapter 5

1. Pat Cloud, "Aliens Stoled My Prewar Mastertone!" From The Pat Cloud Web site (http://www.wmpub.com/PC.html). Originally published in *Pat Cloud, The Adventures of the Original Banjo Answerman.* Reprinted with permission.

2. See George P. Evans, "Gifts of the Holy Spirit," in Michael Downey, ed., *The New Dictionary of Catholic Spirituality* (Collegeville, Minn.: The Liturgical Press, 1993), 437.

3. *The American Heritage Talking Dictionary* (Cambridge, Mass.: The Learning Company, Inc., 1997).

4. Mark Van Doren, "Slowly, Slowly Wisdom Gathers," in *That Shining Place* (New York: Hill and Wang, 1969), 3.

5. The difficult issue of suicide in general deserves a more extensive treatment than can be provided here. "Grave psychological disturbances, anguish, or grave fear of hardship, suffering, or torture can diminish the responsibility of the one committing suicide," says the *Catechism of the Catholic Church* (n. 2282).

6. André Dubus, *Broken Vessels* (Boston: David R. Godine, 1991), 193–94.

7. Andrew M. Greeley, *The Catholic Imagination* (Berkeley, Calif.: University of California Press, 2000), 1.

8. Francine Prose, *Household Saints* (New York: G. K. Hall, 1981 & 1986).

9. Ibid., 227.

10. G. K. Chesterton, *The Napoleon of Notting Hill* (Mahwah, N.J.: Paulist Press, 1978), 1.

11. Robert Clark, *Mr. White's Confession* (New York: Picador, 1998), 340–41.

12. John McCabe, *Mr. Laurel and Mr. Hardy* (New York: Signet Books, 1966), 138–39.

13. See ibid., 169.

Chapter 6

1. Excerpted from the *American Heritage Talking Dictionary*. Copyright 1997, The Learning Company, Inc. All rights reserved.

2. George P. Evans, "Gifts of the Holy Spirit," in Michael Downey, ed., *The New Dictionary of Catholic Spirituality* (Collegeville, Minn.: The Liturgical Press, 1993), 438.

3. Sean Finnegan, ed., *The Book of Catholic Prayer: Prayers for Every Day and All Occasions* (Chicago: Loyola Press, 2000), 255–56.

4. Zachary Hayes, O.F.M., "Creation," in Michael Downey, ed., *The New Dictionary of Catholic Spirituality* (Collegeville, Minn.: The Liturgical Press, 1993), 241.

5. Matthew Fox, *Original Blessing: A Primer in Creation Spirituality* (Santa Fe, N.M.: Bear & Company, 1983), 28–29.

6. *Catechism of the Catholic Church*, n. 1253.

7. Ibid., no. 1674.

8. Thomas Merton, *New Seeds of Contemplation* (New York: New Directions, 1961), 53.

Chapter 7

1. See Myles M. Bourke, "The Epistle to the Hebrews," in Raymond E. Brown, S.S., et al., eds., *The New Jerome Biblical Commentary* (Englewood Cliffs, N.J.: Prentice-Hall, 1990), 921: "Probably, Heb[rews] is a written homily to which the author has given an epistolary ending."

2. George P. Evans, "Gifts of the Holy Spirit," in Michael Downey, ed., *The New Dictionary of Catholic Spirituality* (Collegeville, Minn.: The Liturgical Press, 1993), 438.

3. *Catechism of the Catholic Church*, n. 40.

4. Ibid., n. 42.

5. Mark Van Doren, *100 Poems* (New York: Hill and Wang, 1967), 51.

6. Nancy Willard, *Things Invisible to See* (New York: Alfred A. Knopf, 1984), 3.

7. Although not an exact quotation, the reference is to Isaiah 64:4: "From ages past no one has heard, no ear has perceived, no eye has seen any God besides you, who works for those who wait for him."

8. See Saint Thomas Aquinas, *Summa Theologiae: A Concise Translation,* Timothy McDermott, ed. (Westminster, Md.: Christian Classics), 26.

9. Kathleen Norris, *Little Girls in Church* (Pittsburgh, Penn.: University of Pittsburgh Press, 1995).

10. Ibid., 10.

11. Ibid., 76.

12. Ibid., 50.

13. Johannes P. Louw, "Fear." In Bruce M. Metzger and Michael D. Coogan, eds., *The Oxford Companion to the Bible* (New York: Oxford University Press, 1993), 225.

14. Ibid., 225.

15. See the *Catechism of the Catholic Church,* n. 97: "'Sacred Tradition and Sacred Scripture make up a single sacred deposit of the Word of God' [Vatican II, *Dei Verbum* 10]."

Chapter 8

1. Rev. Peter Klein, ed., *Catholic Source Book* (Dubuque, Iowa: Brown Roa Publishing Media, 1990), 70.

2. See John S. Kselman, "Vulgate," in Richard P. McBrien, general editor, *The HarperCollins Encyclopedia of Catholicism* (San Francisco: HarperSanFrancisco, 1995), 1320.

3. Taken from an Internet source: http://www.hti.umich.edu/relig/rheims/

4. Doctor Joseph Stemler, quoted in Boniface Hanley, O.F.M., *Ten Christians* (Notre Dame, Ind.: Ave Maria Press, 1979), 117.

5. See Kabat-Zinn, Jon. *Wherever You Go, There You Are: Mindfulness Meditation in Everyday Life* (New York: Hyperion, 1994).

6. Excerpted from the *American Heritage Talking Dictionary.* Copyright 1997, The Learning Company. All rights reserved.